"*Conquer Your Deli*, heaven's war room f written another spirit ~~~ ~~~classic that unleashes practical rules-of-engagement strategies to win in this invisible battle against the forces of evil to live in total freedom in Christ."

Dr. Hakeem Collins, international speaker and author, *10 Prayer Secrets* and *Unseen Warfare*

"John Ramirez encourages every believer and leader in the Christian faith to walk in the overwhelming power of the one true living God. He reveals the secrets of the demonic and encourages us to live as an overcoming kingdom of priests. Let the Lion of Judah roar!"

Dr. Candice Smithyman, host, *Glory Road*

"When you've come out of something because of the absolute goodness and mercy of Jesus, you are compelled to share the keys you've learned for freedom with all who will listen. In John Ramirez's book *Conquer Your Deliverance*, you'll gain a ring full of keys and principles to conquer any darkness still at work in your life. Be sure to purchase a few copies of this book, one for you and more for your friends."

Jennifer Eivaz, co-pastor, Harvest Church; founder, Harvest Ministries International; author, *The Intercessors Handbook* and *Seeing the Supernatural*

"*Conquer Your Deliverance* will challenge how you see spiritual warfare and your personal role in your victory. John Ramirez offers riveting parallels and practical strategies from the Word of God that will empower your prayers, build your confidence and give you a road map to freedom. His personal experiences make him a leading voice of victorious living through the power of Jesus Christ!"

Terrell Fletcher, author, *The Book of You*; senior pastor, City of Hope International Church; former NFL running back

CONQUER
YOUR
DELIVERANCE

CONQUER YOUR DELIVERANCE

HOW TO LIVE A LIFE OF TOTAL FREEDOM

JOHN RAMIREZ

Chosen
a division of Baker Publishing Group
Minneapolis, Minnesota

© 2021 by John Ramirez

Published by Chosen Books
11400 Hampshire Avenue South
Bloomington, Minnesota 55438
www.chosenbooks.com

Chosen Books is a division of
Baker Publishing Group, Grand Rapids, Michigan

Printed in the United States of America

Library of Congress Cataloging-in-Publication Data
Names: Ramirez, John, author.
Title: Conquer your deliverance : how to live a life of total freedom / John Ramirez.
Description: Minneapolis, Minnesota : Chosen Books, [2021]
Identifiers: LCCN 2021015687 | ISBN 9780800762506 (casebound) | ISBN 9780800761844 (paperback) | ISBN 9781493433575 (ebook)
Subjects: LCSH: Spiritual warfare.
Classification: LCC BV4509.5 .R355 2021 | DDC 235/.4—dc23
LC record available at https://lccn.loc.gov/2021015687

Cover design by LOOK Design Studio

Author is represented by Leticia Gomez, Savvy Literary Services, and Raoul Davis, Director of Ascendant Publishing.

21 22 23 24 25 26 27   7 6 5 4 3 2 1

Many of us in our lifetimes have someone we look up to. It could be a sports figure, a movie star, a music artist. Many times we go back to our childhoods, and we love our superheroes. For some that is Superman; some might say Spider-Man or even Batman. In my neighborhood, there was no role model. In my home, my hero was absent, which was my father. So along this thing called life, down the path called Journey, I was looking for my hero in all the wrong places. Even in the devil's den.

But one day to my surprise, I met this man—the ultimate Person—who can change your life. Not a temporary transformation; it is an eternal one. This man walked by the Sea of Galilee one day and saw fishermen fishing, and He turned them into fishers of men. This man turned water into wine, walked on water, shut down the storms on a boat by His spoken word: "Peace, be still." He is a miracle worker: With two fish and five loaves of bread He fed more than five thousand people. He had compassion on the sick, gave sight to the blind, even raised the dead. And He was pretty good at His trade of being a carpenter, not knowing that one day they would create a cross out of wood with His name on it, on which He would be crucified.

But that was not His end; it was just the beginning. He was placed in a grave, and on the third day He rose again and spoke to a woman while dressed as a gardener. And she called Him *Rabbi*, which means "teacher."

I am so blessed and so honored and beyond grateful that the man who came out of the tomb did not stay in the garden that day. He knew my address in the Bronx and knocked on my door and not only changed my life, but transformed it forever.

He is my hero, and I dedicate this book to Him.
His name is Jesus Christ, the one and only.

Contents

Foreword

John Ramirez has a truly remarkable story of conquering his battles and experiencing true freedom. The power of his story keeps you on the edge of your seat. Remember that Revelation 12:11 KJV says, "They overcame him by the blood of the Lamb, and by the word of their testimony; and they loved not their lives unto the death."

John has spent years conquering demonic principalities so that you can spend mere moments and days conquering them. By understanding how to renew your mind and access the power of the precious blood of Jesus, you too will experience true freedom.

This topic is more vital now than ever before in human history. Why? Because so many Christians start following Jesus but remain bound in their minds, not knowing how to walk in their God-given authority. I believe true spiritual warfare is the battle for who or what is going to control your thought life and the decision-making center of your life.

I have personally been teaching about the battle of the mind for more than thirty years. Through our podcast, *Ask the Pastor*; television broadcast, *Power to Change Today*; and global

Life Changers Church family, I have seen firsthand how people can be set free by applying the principles of God's Word that John and I teach about.

One of the things I love most about John's approach is when he says, "Say this out loud." There is power in your words! Hebrews 4:12 NIV says, "For the word of God is alive and active. Sharper than any double-edged sword, it penetrates even to dividing soul and spirit, joints and marrow; it judges the thoughts and attitudes of the heart." Did you know the phrase *double-edged sword* is literally translated as "twice spoken"? Think about that. The power of God's Word is activated when it is spoken twice—first, by God, when it was written, and second, by you, when you declare it out loud. The devil has *no* power over you when you come to understand this reality.

Freedom begins when you say what God says about you: "I am the head, not the tail; above only and not beneath" (see Deuteronomy 28:13). Conquering begins when you declare, "I am more than a conqueror." When you believe and speak the Living Word of God, it judges and condemns the things that are judging and condemning you.

However you found yourself opening the pages of this book and entering this personal journey to freedom and deliverance, I believe that your steps were ordered by the Lord.

May you go forward and experience the freedom Jesus paid so dearly for you to have.

It's time to be transformed, starting today. Your best days are your next days!

Gregory Dickow, author, *Fast from Wrong Thinking*;
host, *Power to Change Today*

A Tribute to My Sister, Desiree

And to All the Foster Kids in the World

My sister was born March 20, 1991, and entered the Lord's presence on December 31, 2020.

I remember as a little boy, in my mom's house, my brothers and I would share precious moments in front of the television with foster kids she took into our home. We would sit across from each other with the TV on, watching cartoons and sharing snacks together. My home was a humble beginning, as my daddy was on public assistance. My mom would get a check once a month and feed my brothers and me and our foster family. I always wondered, sitting across from the new foster family, what would possess a mother to give up her kids. No matter how difficult things were in my house, or the things we lacked, my mother loved us and would never give us up.

My brothers and I wanted to share that same love with the foster kids who were sharing our home. We never wanted them to feel as though they lived in a foster home. We loved and we fought, but at the end of the night we had each other's back. We grew up in this kind of home. My mother was our hero.

Not even once did she make them feel like outsiders, or that they were foster children. They were loved unconditionally.

As we grew up, it broke our hearts when they had to leave to go to another house, and we started again with another group of kids who came in. We embraced them as if they were our own family. We missed them and cried when they left.

And that is how Desiree arrived, given to us as a precious gift. When she came in as a baby, my mom bought her a secondhand crib, and we called her our sister from that very first day. Time went by, and her presence and love in the home grew so strong that my mother adopted her. I like to think that all the kids who came in through that door were adopted into our family. Today I stop and rejoice, knowing that Jesus Christ adopted all of us, too, into His family, no matter the different walks of life, the challenges and circumstances we come from. What a blessing!

As I share my heart with you today, I am broken beyond words. Writing this story is one of the hardest things I have ever put on paper. Through no fault of her own, Desiree was born to natural parents who were heroin-addicted, and because her mother was HIV positive, Desiree was born that way, too. Not once did we make her feel any different in our family. Throughout the years, my sister had her challenges with this sickness in her body, but we rallied together and stood with her through thick and thin, through the ups and downs. From hospital to hospital, we were there with her, cheering her on because she was an overcomer.

We kept pushing forward as the years went by, standing strong for Desiree. We loved, we laughed and we cried. That is what family is all about. One thing I have to say about my sister: Even though HIV was her enemy, many times the doctor's report throughout the years told us that this might be her last year. But Desiree was a fighter in her spirit. Sometimes manifestation does not have to be all about demons manifesting to conquer your victory over a satanic plague like HIV.

My sister pushed and fought the good fight and proved the doctor's report to be wrong time after time. We laughed and celebrated those beautiful days, weeks and years. God is good.

To all the foster kids throughout the world, no matter what home you have been placed in, know one thing: The Lord Jesus Christ loves you and knows right where you are, and He has a wonderful plan for you. My sister proved to the medical field that HIV had nothing on her, even to the point that later she had two beautiful daughters of her own. And God is a miracle-working God: Her daughters were born without HIV. What a gift!

My sister shined bright throughout the years and had her moments that were dim, too, but no devil, no hell, no sickness was able to turn off the candle of hope. She stood the test; she took the class and got the passing grade. She lived with her two daughters and was an incredible mother. Oddly enough, even though her natural parents were not role models, our humble home where she grew up became the place where she was nurtured and learned how to be a mother herself, from my own mother. Desiree is a hero.

It is amazing how God works in mysterious ways.

Isaiah 55:8–9 (NIV) says, "'For my thoughts are not your thoughts, neither are your ways my ways,' declares the LORD. 'As the heavens are higher than the earth, so are my ways higher than your ways and my thoughts than your thoughts.'"

One day a couple of years ago my mom called me—my sister was 27 years old—and said, "Desiree is sick, and she's not doing well. Can you call her and pray for her?" I remember it as if it happened yesterday. I called her up and prayed with her on the phone. At that moment I felt the Holy Spirit prompt me to ask her to receive Jesus as her Lord and Savior, and we said the sinner's prayer together that day. What a powerful day that was!

In December 2020, my sister got sick again and was rushed to the hospital at four in the morning, leaving her home in a desperate moment, not knowing if she would ever return and see her daughters again. As my sister went to the hospital where she eventually died, the grace of God brought her back again. I prayed my heart out for her to be healed, and I had seasoned intercessors and a few other godly people join me in prayer. Every day we prayed. We stormed heaven; we put on our spiritual-warfare garments and attacked every sickness and premature death off of my sister. On December 31, at 7:09 p.m., my mother sat in the hospital holding her hand. My beautiful sister was only 29 years old. As my mother held her hand, my sister slipped into eternity. She went straight from the hands of a wonderful mother into the hands of Jesus.

My baby sister, Desiree Rivera Ramirez, I am not saying good-bye, but I am saying I will see you later. I love you and will miss you. Thank you for being a gift to my family.

God is good. He kept my sister here for 29 years. Her true purpose was to bless the family with two beautiful girls, HIV free, and to say yes to Jesus and make heaven her home.

To all the foster children in the world, you are a gift from God, just like my sister, Desiree. Say this prayer with me, the same one that Desiree prayed some time ago:

Lord Jesus, I know that I was born a sinner, but I do not have to stay this way because You died on the cross for me. Forgive me for all of my sins, come into my life and be my Lord and Savior. The same way You came into Desiree's life, come into mine, in Jesus' name.

Hey, Desiree, I know you are in heaven, and you can hear me. This is your big brother. When people say this prayer, these souls will belong to you and will be credited to you in heaven.

Even though when you were alive on the earth you didn't get the opportunity to win souls, now you do. Glory to God! We are going to miss you like crazy!

Your big brother,
John Ramirez

See you again one day.

Why I Want You to Read This Book

I dedicate this book to the brothers and sisters who have been spiritually wounded. I promise one thing—that your spiritual wounds are not your destination but rather are preparing and equipping you for a deeper place in God. You will have the last laugh against the enemy of your soul. I know that in the past, you have seen the goodness of God upon your life. As you look back—something the enemy does not want you or me to do— the Holy Spirit wants you not only to remember the amazing things He did in your past, but also to expect in the present the things that our Lord Jesus Christ has predestined for you. Things He did in the past will be outdone only by what He has promised to do for you and me in these precious times.

God has a plan for you. Yes, believe it. And it is a big one, an amazing and perfect plan. The powers of darkness, the devil and his army, do not want your God-ordained purpose and destiny to be fulfilled in your life. In this very hour, he has mobilized his demons, both his generals and satanic spirits—and even human agents of the devil that are doing his bidding—to launch the most ferocious attack against you and me and every human being because we are made in the very image of God.

The world has seen up to this point what is coming down the pipeline against believers and nonbelievers alike, straight from the pits of hell. We have seen satanic strategies on every level. But I have good news for you. The true servants of Jesus Christ will be prayed up and filled with the Word of God to withstand and be more than conquerors—soldiers who have been enlisted in the army of the Lord and deployed into the battlefield behind enemy lines, like never before.

It is time we pick up the weapons of our warfare and bring them to the devil—instead of just talking about it—if we want to experience the type of victory Jesus already purchased for us through the finished work of the cross. Wake up, Church, from your slumber. One thing I know about the enemy, after spending 25 years in the devil's camp, is that he is strong and relentless. He is swift and experienced in the battle. But there is a power he cannot break or destroy. He does not have any authority against the true believer in Christ; he cannot overthrow this power. There is a name and power that is above every other name and every other power of the satanic world, in this world and in the world to come, and that all-powerful name is *Jesus Christ*. I am going to shout my hallelujah!

I believe in my heart that in every generation God calls a person to move on His behalf. I thank God that in 1999, when I lived in a neighborhood with 179 buildings, out of all those dwellings in the burnt-out Bronx He knew my address that night, and I answered the call of spiritual warfare. I am moved in my spirit to equip the saints of God for such a time as this, by the power of the Holy Spirit, to overthrow the powers of the demonic world—the devil, his principalities and every satanic warlock and witch serving as agent of the kingdom of darkness—to break curses and satanic manipulation and control over our lives, our homes, our marriages, our children, our finances, our relationships, our ministries, our churches, our careers, our health and our purpose and destiny. I pray that we be equipped to destroy every hindering, blocking, robbing spirit, and every assignment of the devil, every dark area, whether it is from a generational curse or from a door we opened that gave the devil legal rights. It is time to bring them down once and for all as you take this journey with me through *Conquer Your Deliverance: How to Live a Life of Total Freedom.*

As you engage the enemy and pray the powerful prayer points in this book, pray them with Holy Spirit fire, full of faith and expecting that your prayers will destroy the satanic powers of the devil and his cronies, in the spirit realm, at the very moment you release the arsenals of heaven upon their heads. I declare and decree that your prayers will carry the power of the almighty God. The Holy Spirit will lead you into the battlefield of your life, and He will lead you into total victory. I guarantee you mighty victory in Jesus' name.

Get ready for the battle! Put on your armor, pick up your spiritual weapons and begin to confront what is in front of you, using the prayers of war that are deep down in your spirit. Release them now in the unmatchable name of Jesus Christ. Amen.

21

Introduction

A fable is told about an eagle who grew up thinking he was a chicken. When he was just an eaglet, he fell from his nest, and a chicken farmer, wanting to save his life, brought him home and raised him on his chicken farm. The eagle grew up learning how to live like a chicken, believing he was a chicken.

A naturalist came to the farm to see this "eagle turned chicken." He knew eagles were beautiful creatures, kings of the sky. To his wonder, the eagle was indeed strutting around the chicken coop, pecking at the ground, acting like a chicken. The naturalist knew that being born an eagle, he had the heart of an eagle and nothing, not even how he was raised, could change that. Picking up the eagle, he placed him on the fence surrounding the chicken coop and encouraged him to "stretch forth his wings and fly."

The eagle looked at the man, then at the farmer, and finally at his coop mates and his comfortable surroundings. He jumped off the fence and continued doing what chickens do. This same scenario continued several more times, and despite the naturalist's best efforts to convince the eagle he was born for something greater, he continued to remain content in the chicken coop.

Asking the farmer if he could try one more time, the naturalist took the eagle and the farmer far away from the chicken coop, to the foot of a high mountain. No one could see the farm or coop from this distance, at which point the farmer held the eagle on his arm and pointed up in the sky toward the sun.

"Eagle, thou art an eagle! Thou dost belong to the sky and not to the earth. Stretch forth thy wings and fly."

This time the eagle straightened his large body, stretched his massive wings and—moving slowly at first, but with steadily increasing strength—flew away with a screech. He had finally believed what the naturalist knew all along: He was an eagle and destined for so much more than scratching and pecking at the ground like a chicken.

Every person who is "born again" is automatically born into a royal priesthood. He or she is now the heavenly Father's son or daughter, adopted into His family. But, similar to the eagle in the fable above, Christians have a choice to make. They can either stay chained up in the chicken coop, pecking, whining and complaining about their circumstances, or choose to soar to great heights as the eagles God designed them to be.

Chicken-coop Christians do not seek growth. They rely on others to fight for them, refusing to learn the skills needed for battle. They stay weak, young and immature.

Eagles, however, are amazing creatures. They were created with two sets of eyelids, and, while flying, they close one set to help with vision by keeping dust and debris away.

God created His children to be eagle Christians. We are going to go through battles in life; Jesus tells His disciples this: "In this world you will have trouble" (John 16:33 NIV). Eagle Christians are those who close their eyes to the flesh (first eyelids) but keep their spiritual eyes open (second eyelids), asking God to equip them for the battles ahead and praising Him for the strength He will provide to gain victory.

I have been asked multiple times, "How, John, how do I do that?" *Conquer Your Deliverance* is an in-depth look at the key components to maturing from a chicken-coop-Christian perspective to someone who soars to great heights as an eagle, above the defeat of the enemy. You will be surprised at how easy it is to fly when you are equipped with the right perspective.

So the question is, How do we become eagle Christians? Those who will be unshakable and assured, deeply at peace? Because we are certain that trials, temptations and battles will come. Jesus Himself told us that fact. But He also told us to be prepared, and how to get ready. In this book I will come alongside you and show you how to mature in your faith, not only to gain the victory but to be better prepared for your next encounter with the enemy.

1

Getting Off Gilligan's Island

In the 1960s TV show *Gilligan's Island*, Skipper and Gilligan and their five passengers sailed off in a charter boat under blue skies in crystal-blue waters. No one anticipated the typhoon ahead, the storm that would shipwreck them on an unknown Pacific island and change their lives forever. Each week the castaways devised a plan to get off the island. Not one worked.

Gilligan's Island is a metaphor for the Church at large today. So many believers are stuck on an island and cannot get off because somehow what started as a sunny day, receiving Jesus as their Lord and Savior—the most beautiful thing that can happen to any human being in a lifetime—turned dark. The sun disappeared, the clouds came out, the weather changed and before they knew it, reality hit. They became shipwrecked on their own islands, just like the castaways, unable to devise a plan of escape.

What is the name of your island? Despair, torment, unforgiveness, rejection, molestation, rape, generational curses, witchcraft, infirmity? The list is endless. You find no lasting breakthrough, healing or deliverance.

There are three voices that speak to us: our own voice of reason, the voice of the Holy Spirit and the voice of the devil. Which one has your attention? Conquering your deliverance requires you to hear the voice of the Holy Spirit to learn how to maintain the spiritual freedom Jesus purchased for you on the cross.

Now is the time to accept that gift and use your weapons: the power of the Holy Spirit, declarations and decrees partnered with targeted prayers, and the faith deposited in your own heart. This threefold combination, a God-given strategy, is His plan to set you free once and for all.

It is time to get off the island.

Castaways No More

For 25 years, the name of my island was "Devil's Island," and on this island lived rejection. I had no love from my father, had a mother who was beat up all the time, lived in poverty and cried oceans of tears. Thanks be to God that in 1999 I got off my island because Jesus Christ showed up in His boat.

Many good brothers and sisters come to Jesus but never get off their islands. On *Gilligan's Island*, the castaways tried every trick in the book to get off the island, on every episode, whether building a raft or throwing a bottle with a message into the lagoon—you name it. Every human effort and man-made invention made it look as if they were going to get off the island once and for all. Many of us were cheering them on, and somehow we thought that that was the episode in which they would finally be set free, only to realize that we would tune in the following week to see the same situation play all over again. We experienced the happy and sad moments along with the castaways, the hope and expectation, the emotional highs and lows with every show, but they were still stuck on the island.

This sounds so much like the Church today. In our weekly gatherings, we have incredible worship and good preaching, but at the end of the service many of us are still in the same place spiritually, still on the same old island, just like Gilligan. There is no sign of total freedom.

The Church is depleted the same way Israel was in the days of Nehemiah: The walls are down, and the people are spiritually bankrupt, defeated almost to the point of being destroyed with hopelessness and discouragement.

Leaders today need to take a page from Nehemiah's life, one man seeking God with fasting and prayer and the spirit of anguish. Instead, many leaders today are busy fulfilling the flesh and seeking the inventions of man instead of seeking God to help people get off the island.

The castaways on *Gilligan's Island* heard many voices sharing ideas, but no one had the right idea. Today in the Church at large, we have failed to hear the voice of the Holy Spirit for God's people. I get fifteen thousand email messages a year, and I call them the cries of the Church. Sometimes I feel like Nehemiah, with a spirit of anguish for God's people who are my brothers and sisters that I truly love with all my heart. As the Lord bears witness in my life, I am on Zoom meetings scheduled for two hours that end up being six or seven hours because I hear the heartbeat of brothers and sisters wanting deliverance in order to be set free, and of other brothers and sisters who want to know how to conquer their deliverance and stay free. The Bible says, "My people are destroyed from lack of knowledge" (Hosea 4:6 NIV).

We leaders need to "man up" and hold ourselves accountable, including myself, to be our brothers' keepers. Instead, we all keep living on this island that we call "the church"; no one is getting off spiritually. Week after week, month after month and year after year, in our midweek services and Sunday services, we see the same pattern: no breakthrough, no healing, no deliverance, no spiritual maturity. We are in the same condition as the Israelites in the book of Numbers. They started their journey, but after forty years they grew old but never grew up—they ended up being spiritual corpses. Only two people out of an estimated three million, Joshua and Caleb, were of a "different spirit" and conquered their Promised Land. Many believers today are stuck on the island they call "the church," and only a few conquer their deliverance and move on to the life of total freedom that God preordained for us before the foundations of the world.

The Face of God

In Numbers 6:25 (BSB) we read these astounding words: "May the LORD cause His face to shine upon you and be gracious to you."

I believe that most of us in the Church have the right intentions, but we have let the devil sidetrack us, because while we may be seeking God's way, we are not seeking His face. We will never get off the island because instead of seeking Him, we have created a religion with a New Age Jesus, a powerless Jesus.

Second Corinthians 11:4 (NLT) says, "You happily put up with whatever anyone tells you, even if they preach a different Jesus than the one we preach, or a different kind of Spirit than the one you received, or a different kind of gospel than the one you believed."

Conquering your deliverance means maintaining the opportunity of spiritual freedom that our Lord Jesus Christ paid for in full. He has given us something priceless. It is like walking into a classroom and sitting down, and hearing the teacher or professor tell you on the first day, "I'm going to give you an A." In other words, the day you say yes to Jesus, "Come into my life and be my Lord and Savior," He gives you an A. Through the power of the Holy Spirit and in partnership with Him, our job is to maintain that A. This is what you call conquering your deliverance.

If your A has decreased to a B, C, D or F, it is time to get back to the will of God, of our Lord Jesus Christ. Whether you struggle with generational curses or besetting sins (things you think have gone away but keep coming back) or gateways and portals you have opened, giving the enemy of your soul legal rights to your A, it is time to get off Gilligan's Island. We are going to come into agreement and declare and decree these powerful prayers, in the power of the Holy Spirit and with the faith that our Lord Jesus Christ has already deposited in our hearts. We are going to mix these together, and you will be set free.

Prayer to Be Armed and Dangerous

Say this with me with now:

> *I decree right now, in the name of our Lord Jesus Christ: Devil, I put you on notice that the Pharaoh I see today in your army of demons, I will see no more. I am seated with Jesus Christ in the third heaven, and I am attacking you, devil, from my place of authority over the spiritual realm and the kingdom of darkness. The Lord has made me armed and dangerous through the power of the Holy Spirit, in Jesus' name.*

2

More Than a
"Get Out of Hell Free" Card

Today we are living in what I call the error of the Church. We have told the world that if you come to Jesus and receive the free gift of salvation, all generational curses in your family, and any spiritual open doors or gateways or portals you might have opened, knowingly or unknowingly, will fall off automatically.

I see this everywhere I go in my ministry travels.

Many times people accept the free gift of salvation and ask Jesus to be in charge of their lives. They assume the battle is over and that by praying the sinner's prayer they have their "get out of hell free" card. But in actuality the battle has just begun. This is the kind of mind-set that many in the Church have contaminated the believer with, only to realize later that the real battle is just beginning.

Believers need to get prepared and equipped because the enemy plays for keeps. When the Church fails to break, destroy and dismantle the spiritual walls of depression, oppression, unforgiveness, bitterness, resentment and suicide (to name a few), these spiritual walls will block you from having a closer relationship with the Lord Jesus Christ, by the power of the Holy Spirit.

The Big Deception

The Church at large is under the big deception that once we get saved, every stronghold of the devil falls away automatically, when we have not even dealt with the first walls. Then we unknowingly build more spiritual walls to protect ourselves from the enemy. These are the very walls that the enemy uses against us. This is what the devil calls spiritual incarceration.

The Church talks about the enemy but never confronts the enemy. We lack spiritual-warfare tactics and spiritual-warfare training, and we also lack understanding of the arsenals of heaven because we do not have the faith to confront the devil. We use words like *claim it*, *grab it* and *receive it by faith*. This is fake Christianity, which is equivalent to fake news and is far from the truth of who Jesus Christ is. Fake news is something repeated so many times that it starts to sound real, but it is not real to God. This mind-set is unbiblical and demonic.

Who did more spiritual warfare in the Bible than Jesus Christ? He healed the sick, gave sight to the blind and cast out demons. The Church needs to wake up and be the Church. You will never be delivered, or conquer your deliverance, if you never confront the enemy head on with the power of the Holy Spirit.

It is time to get rid of the fantasy we are living in, because the devil is real, and he comes to kill, steal and destroy—but our Lord Jesus Christ has come to set the captives free. He left the Church here to do the same exact thing, but we have drifted far to the left, off the pages of the Bible. We no longer live like the real Church, like the early Church in the book of Acts. We have replaced the real Church and have become the medicated

Church. We medicate ourselves with false theology, false doctrine and a New Age Bible. Sad to say, many believers today, instead of getting the deliverance they deserve, are drowning in prescriptions and pills. You cannot medicate a demon; it needs to be cast out.

Now we have created a new "church" that is called seeker friendly and politically correct. We do not want the Gospel of Jesus Christ to offend anyone, or to bring conviction, or to challenge sin in any way. We make it cozy, comfortable and easy for the people of God. We say, "You can come just the way you are and stay the way you are," instead of saying, "Come as you are and let God change you." We sell fake joy and peace to sugarcoat the condition of those who come, while they remain spiritually in the intensive care unit.

Make a decision today and let the devil know whose side you are really on. Either you are on a cruise-ship church pleasing the devil, or you are on the battleship Church going the distance with Jesus. Most Christians are bunny-hopping from one church building to another, looking for a fix to get spiritually high—in other words, to be entertained, but never transformed. We are losing the battle as ministers and leaving our brothers and sisters wounded on the battlefield. Call me Mr. Monopoly, because I have your "get out of jail free" card: I want to help get you out of a fake relationship with Jesus and bring you into a real relationship with Him.

Here is the résumé of an ex-murderer who became the great apostle Paul. What would your résumé say, or what do you want it to say about you?

Whatever anyone else dares to boast about—I am speaking as a fool—I also dare to boast about. Are they Hebrews? So am I. Are they Israelites? So am I. Are they Abraham's descendants? So am I. Are they servants of Christ? (I am out of my mind to

34

talk like this.) I am more. I have worked much harder, been in prison more frequently, been flogged more severely, and been exposed to death again and again. Five times I received from the Jews the forty lashes minus one. Three times I was beaten with rods, once I was pelted with stones, three times I was shipwrecked, I spent a night and a day in the open sea, I have been constantly on the move. I have been in danger from rivers, in danger from bandits, in danger from my fellow Jews, in danger from Gentiles; in danger in the city, in danger in the country, in danger at sea; and in danger from false believers. I have labored and toiled and have often gone without sleep; I have known hunger and thirst and have often gone without food; I have been cold and naked. Besides everything else, I face daily the pressure of my concern for all the churches. Who is weak, and I do not feel weak? Who is led into sin, and I do not inwardly burn?

If I must boast, I will boast of the things that show my weakness. The God and Father of the Lord Jesus, who is to be praised forever, knows that I am not lying.

2 Corinthians 11:21–31 NIV

Stay Hungry, Stay Thirsty

I would like to share a word from my résumé. I learned from the very beginning of my Christian walk not to settle for a mediocre Church of our Lord Jesus Christ. In my earlier walk with the Lord, I started with a church community that was on fire. Later it lost its flame. I cried out to God, "Is this what You have for me? Mediocre Christianity? You should have left me where I was as a devil worshiper." I was hungry and thirsty to go deeper with God.

The words of Psalm 42:7 (NIV) spoke of my heart: "Deep calls to deep in the roar of your waterfalls; all your waves and breakers have swept over me."

That is how I felt when that precious church lost its fire, and I was left in the middle of nowhere. Sometime later the Lord sent me to Times Square Church, where I had the honor to meet Pastor David Wilkerson and also be mentored by him. To my surprise, I had an opportunity to meet Nicky Cruz, one of the greatest evangelists of our time, and he has inspired my life greatly. I thank God for his ministry. The list goes on of the incredible blessings the Lord has blessed me with.

On the other side of my résumé is the story of pain and betrayal from brothers and sisters in the Church against me. (I will go into this story in more detail later.) I went hungry for three years, lost my finances, lost my home and, on top of that, I later lost my eyesight for over three months. I was registered with the Commissioner of the Blind of New York State.

Through all this, I was still seeking Jesus, and I never gave up, nor did I ever give in.

Do Not Settle for the Spirit of This Age

When the whispers of the enemy came in the night that I was done and had no ministry, the voice also said that Jesus did not love me. I would stop the devil in his tracks and say to him, "I promise you that I will have the last laugh. I will still trust in Him who has called me from the place of death into His marvelous light."

I was bleeding spiritually, left for dead on the side of the road and could not afford a meal at a restaurant, but I refused to surrender my peace and joy and trust in the Lord. I did not settle for a New Age Jesus, and I did not sit in a dead church. I did not buy into a fake theology or false doctrine of "come to Jesus and everything will be peaches and cream," believing that all the devil-worshiping ceremonies and contracts would automatically fall off me. I came dirty and filthy spiritually. I came as I was and allowed the hand of God to transform me.

I took the narrow road that leads to life. I rested on the finished work of the cross of Jesus Christ. This can be your story today.

Jeremiah 29:11 says this: "'I know the plans I have for you,' declares the LORD, 'plans to prosper you and not to harm you, plans to give you hope and a future.'"

It is time to stop drinking the Kool-Aid, get off the cruiseship church, jump into the battleship Church and start moving into the purpose and destiny that God has for you.

I love you so much, my brother and sister. The truth will set us free.

3

God Loves the Misfit

Jeremiah 29:11 (NIV) says this: "'I know the plans I have for you,' declares the LORD, 'plans to prosper you and not to harm you, plans to give you hope and a future.'" And in Jeremiah 1:5 (NIV) we read: "Before I formed you in the womb I knew you, before you were born I set you apart."

We live between two worlds, the physical and spiritual realms, and no one knows the full spectrum of these two worlds but God. We, as people, started our journeys in a place called heaven. One day we had an incredible meeting in the throne room of heaven with God discussing the plans for our lives, the purposes and destinies that He ordained for us. In this journey called *life*, the prize of eternity is to get back home with God, to the place we started from.

Our birthdates were given, our families were chosen and we came into existence. We were given a timeline to finish our missions. In fact, the only thing that God left out from telling us was the time and day of when we die. We do not pick Mama or Daddy, we do not pick the journey and we do not even pick the neighborhood. We are appointed to the journey by God.

I believe that the day we are born, God blesses us with a guardian angel to lead the way. But the enemy also sends a demon to torment us, whether through the generational curses in our families or the bad decisions we make along the way. We live in this world, called the earth, but we are citizens of heaven. As my friend Juan Martinez of Get Wrapped Church says, we are "Heavicans"—from heaven with a unique passport. The devil's scheme is to steal your passport so you will not get back home.

Let the journey begin.

The Perfect Reject

Mine started in Puerto Rico and soon transitioned when my parents immigrated to the United States, to a borough in New York called the South Bronx. I was born into a crazy world to a crazy family and was placed in a crazy neighborhood. My one-liner has always been, "You are better off in the Bronx Zoo with the animals than with the people I grew up with."

I was handpicked at the age of seven by the second heaven, where the principalities and demonic powers reside, through a necklace with the seven demonic powers that dropped at my feet. As an innocent little boy, I took the bait from the principalities that day. Not long after, at the age of eight, my mother held me by the hand and took me with my aunt to a witch's house. No decision of my own; I was just tagging along, not knowing that I was stepping into the unseen world of the devil's kingdom through an initiation of tarot card reading. Seven days later, I found myself doing my first demonic ceremony.

A world I would never wish upon anyone, not even my worst enemy, unfolded before me. I know God loves the misfit. I lived in the shadow places—shattered with brokenness, emptiness, darkness, no direction, no love of my dad and a broken mother (physically, spiritually, emotionally and mentally). My life was spiritually incarcerated. I stepped into quicksand. My brothers and I were victims of our father's demise and his demonic world. The bloodline of witchcraft followed us all the way from Puerto Rico to the United States.

I recall the unpainted walls of an almost empty apartment that I lived in with my family, with broken furniture, an empty fridge and an almost empty closet with few hangers. My mother and brothers also had pain, rejection, shame, hurt and demons.

I remember the times when my father, who was a warlock, sent me to the witchcraft store. I would run down the stairs and bypass the elevator into the dingy hallway. The walls were dark and the floors were dirty in that six-story building, and I would emerge from the darkness into the bright daylight outside, running down the street, dodging the cars across the avenue to cross the street.

I was out of breath once I reached the witchcraft store, only because I wanted to impress my dad and hear the words I longed to hear: "Well done, my son. I love you so much." I gasped to hear those words at least once out of my dad's mouth. The only words that came out of his mouth cut like a razor blade, shredding me to pieces: "You're stupid, you're dumb, you will never be nothing." His words pierced right through my soul and left me hollow, fragmented and crushed as a young boy.

I would stop to think from time to time and hope that one day my dad would come to his senses—just once—and say that he loved me and my brothers from the bottom of his heart. I would have paid or given anything in this world to hear those words. We wished to see that day, but it never came. My dad's life ended abruptly one night when he was 33 years old. He was shot in the face and died instantly at a bar fighting over a woman who was not his, while he had an amazing wife at home. Those words never came to pass. But God loves the misfit.

The Bible says in Psalm 23:4 (NIV), "Even though I walk through the darkest valley, I will fear no evil, for you are with me; your rod and your staff, they comfort me."

As I grew up, throughout my youth and teenage years, making pacts with the demons and doing ceremonies and rituals and attending demon church, somehow I met a girl. We got married on Halloween because we wanted to please the devil. We had one of the most diabolical ceremonies you could ever imagine, held in a dark basement. You could feel the unseen world as the devil waited for the ceremony to begin. The aura and presence of this monster waited in the shadows to initiate the wedding ceremony. Mediums, witches and warlocks were also there, attending my demonic wedding to bless it.

But God loves the misfit.

Sometime later, on June 28, 1989, my daughter was born into a crazy, satanic family called Ramirez. Little did my daughter know that what goes around comes around. She was born into these demonic generational curses. The Bible says there is nothing new under the sun. History repeated itself, and somehow my upbringing became my daughter's life. It was like hitting the rewind button. She grew up with a warlock father and got initiated into the dark side, just as I was with my own father. She had a messed-up father, just as I did. A demonic upbringing, just like the one I had. Through no fault of her own.

Years later, divorce knocked on my door; mine was a physical divorce whereas my father's "divorce" had been death. It is funny: The person I hated with all my heart, life and guts, I became an exact duplicate of. I was a copycat of everything he was. Every time I looked in the mirror, I did not see myself; I saw my dad.

But God loves the misfit.

The Masterpiece

I heard once that as you write your own story, you are going to need a lot of white-out. But if you let God hold the pen, He can write a masterpiece. He can make a number-one bestseller, an amazing symphony of your life.

As I moved through the dark pages of my own book, strutting through life, I came to a place where I sold my soul to the devil and performed on my body and head every satanic ritual a person can ever do. I guess they call that "from the top of your head to the soles of your feet." Drenched in satanic rituals, I looked brand new on the outside but was hollow and empty on the inside, like a graveyard. I sold my soul on a diabolical night in October with seventeen other attendees who were doing the same thing. As I approached the door of the basement of my aunt's house for the ceremony, I could hear the demonic drumbeats play. It was like walking into the doors of hell, to the point of no return. High-ranked warlocks waited inside for us to enter the room. We were blindfolded, and it was time to let the games begin.

You might not believe this, but I could actually hear the footsteps of the devil coming in at midnight to claim our souls. Out of the seventeen demonic disciples, I was the only one selected by the devil. The leading warlock carved a pentagram and the symbols of the 21 rules of the dark side into my flesh with a one-edged razor. I clenched my teeth as blood ran down the side of my arm, determined not to faint. Because of the massive loss of blood, many of the other demonic disciples passed out. I was the only one left standing that night and slept practically naked on that cold cement floor, into the morning, to finish off my demonic contract.

I no longer owned my own soul. The devil owned it one hundred percent. A season later, I finished my demonic race, accomplishing all the ceremonies that a human being can undergo in the devil's kingdom. The last ceremony was a Haitian ritual that ended with an ice-cold bucket of water thrown over my head. It flowed down to the soles of my feet to seal the deal.

Later, as a believer in Jesus Christ, it broke my heart to witness many members of the Church of Jesus Christ practice this same ceremony, which is called the Ice Bucket Challenge.

But that night, after that last ceremony, I felt like Superman with an *S* on my chest and a cape on my back, wearing my red boots. I felt untouchable. God loves the misfit, but we know that even Superman has a weakness called kryptonite. I cruised through life in the demonic world, astral projecting and attending demon church and every club in NYC to recruit people into the devil's kingdom.

One day after clubbing, the kryptonite finally hit me in front of my television when the voice of God spoke to me. Never in my 25 years of devil worshiping had I ever heard His voice, but that morning an audible voice said to me, *My son, I'm coming soon. What are you going to do with yourself?*

I was hit so hard it shook me like a leaf. I knew the voice of every demonic spirit and the devil himself. But this voice was different. In that instant, I knew beyond the shadow of a doubt that this was the voice of Jesus Christ. The voice had authority like no voice I had ever heard before, yet it carried peace that would shake the earth. It had a love sound to it that you could not deny.

God loves the misfit.

A short time later, I found myself wrestling with God, sitting on my bed. As the night drifted by, I was pleading and saying to Him, "I don't want to be a Christian! I would rather die and go to hell than betray the [occult] religion and the devil, because Christians are weak."

Eventually I fell into a deep sleep as if from anesthesia. In my dream I was on a crowded train, hell-bound. The fear that wrapped around us could never compare to any type of fear we experienced on earth. An elegant woman demon on the train, which Christians call Jezebel, pierced me with her dark eyes. She looked right through my eyes directly to my soul, and called me a traitor in demonic tongues. As the train exploded into hell and the doors opened, I stepped out and knew with all my heart that it was hell. I did not need to question it. Hell is the absence of God. The ground there breathed like a human being, like something alive. I saw people in hell who were in the occult and still living on the earth.

As I ran through the portals of hell, trying to find my way out, demonic fear wrapped around me like a straitjacket. I could not gather my thoughts. All I knew was that I did not belong there. As I confronted my "daddy"—the devil I had served for 25 years—he became angry beyond any human comprehension. As he went to grab me, to try to destroy me, the old rugged wooden cross showed up out of nowhere and defeated the enemy of my soul.

As I ran to another part of hell, trying to find my escape, the devil appeared again and was even more ferocious. As he went to grab me for his last time ever, the cross appeared once again and dropped the enemy of my soul to his knees as though he was nothing. I do not know how I ended up back in my body, but it was like being in the ICU and having electrical paddles on my chest to revive me.

That night I gave my life to Jesus Christ. After 25 years, I gave up on the daddy I was able to see (the devil) for a daddy I could not see, but He touched me.

God loves the misfit.

Ham-and-Cheese Sandwich

This former devil worshiper was now a believer and follower of Jesus Christ.

It is not where you start but where you finish. I remember one summer night my friend Jose, who was also my discipleship teacher, was going with his family to a Christian event at Flushing Meadows Park in Queens, New York. At the time, I never got much attention in the Church to go anywhere with anyone.

Flashback to a quick story. On an early Saturday afternoon, some of the guys in the church I attended invited me to go with them to return some tuxedos for a wedding they had attended the night before. To my surprise I said yes and drove along with them. We jumped into a beat-down burgundy minivan so out of date I was surprised it was still moving.

There were seven of us in the van that day. All I heard were shouts of "Hallelujah, praise the Lord!" as I sat looking out the window in the back of the van, thinking, *Get me out of here.*

One of the guys turned to me and said, "John, what was your take on the service last week?"

I was shocked and embarrassed and had no idea what to say. With my face red, I said, "I don't know." All I was thinking was, why would they invite me to return the tuxedo but not to attend the wedding? That day was very awkward and unpleasant.

God loves the misfit.

Fast-forward. My awesome friend Jose, my discipleship teacher, invited me to an event in Flushing Meadows to see a guy who was preaching that night. I heard he was an evangelist, and his name was Billy Graham. As we made our way to the park, we were trying to find a good spot where we could see the stage. People were coming from everywhere. We found a good spot under a tree, and I sat there on a big rock, waiting for the event to start and wondering what this man called Billy Graham would be preaching that night. It was dusty and hot that evening. As I turned to my friend, he went into his bag filled with goodies and handed me a Coke and a ham-and-cheese sandwich.

It was an amazing night. At the end of the service, people rushed to the altar for salvation. I was blown away to see the gift from God upon this man and how the words that came out of his mouth shook people that night and brought them to the feet of the cross. I can only imagine that maybe one day it would be my turn to do the same.

God loves the misfit.

Life might hit you hard, and you might not get the right deck of cards. You might come from a place of brokenness. Maybe you grew up without a father. Maybe your father was always home and sitting right across from you, but still absent (like mine). Maybe life has thrown you a deathblow, no mother or father, or maybe you grew up in a foster home. My precious mother was a foster parent and took in foster kids when we were growing up. You could see the look in their eyes, coming into the unknown, broken and sad, scared to death, just wanting to be loved. My mom was my hero; she loved these foster kids like her very own.

That is not the case with many. Unfortunately, hurt and pain have followed most of us since birth. Whether you were molested or raped by a family member, or maybe caught up in the world of homosexuality like my brother Jimmy, or spent time in jail, or maybe you have been crushed by the Church . . .

God loves the misfit.

Following Christ Puts You on the Devil's Radar

Have you ever considered what it would have been like to walk in the shoes of King David? Most people, when they think of David, describe him as "a man after God's own heart." In other words, they think of his successes. He killed Goliath when everyone else cowered in fear of the giant bully. He was considered a masterful warrior, winning many battles and always giving God the glory for the victories. He was also the father of Solomon and helped supply financially for the building of God's Temple.

That, however, is not David's full story. He started out as a forgotten shepherd in the fields while his brothers went to fight Goliath and the Philistines. He was overlooked by his own father for the anointing as king; it was only when Samuel asked if Jesse had any other sons that David was called in from the fields, sweaty and dirty and smelling like sheep.

David was a misfit, the one nobody quite knew what to do with. But God saw him and chose him because God loves a misfit.

He was told he would rule the nation someday—but then he was sent back out to tend the sheep because it was not his time yet. He was hired by King Saul, who became jealous of his young protégé. David spent years on the run from the psychopathic Saul, and as a result learned many maneuvers that served him well in the battles he would face when he was eventually crowned king.

If you said yes to Jesus today, I promise you from the bottom of my heart that you will conquer your deliverance through the finished work of the cross, no matter where you find yourself in life. You are not too far gone for the Lord Jesus Christ. It is like the movie *The Shawshank Redemption*, which is based on a true story about a man whose life was turned upside down when he was accused of murdering his wife, a crime he never committed.

How many of us can relate to this story because of how life has treated us? There is someone bigger than life, and His name is Jesus Christ. The beauty of this amazing movie is that the man escaped from his own prison of pain, hurt, despair and tragedy. He swam through a pool of filth and waste and came out clean on the other side, with a new life. This is symbolic of you and me: We can be made clean through Jesus Christ and the finished work of the cross—freed from the filth and pain and broken places of our lives—if we put our trust in Him.

You can conquer your deliverance. Your mess will be a masterpiece because God loves the misfit. This is my story, and it can be yours, too. God loves you.

If you want total freedom, repeat this prayer after me:

Lord Jesus, I know that the Father is not looking for perfect people, and that He is looking for people like me, who are incomplete. I pray today that You will write the story of my life and line me up with Your perfect will. In Jesus' name.

You will find in this book many more prayers of redemption so that you can have the brand-new life that God created for you, because today He wants to write your story. In Jesus' name, Amen.

4

The Devil's Résumé

Before we go deeper, let me tell you a little bit about the devil first so you have a clear picture and understanding in your mind of whom you are fighting against. First of all, the Word of God does not paint the devil as a cartoon character, but the Church does. This is a big mistake. Believers downplay our number-one enemy, but God does not. This is the sort of thing that makes us not take the devil seriously. The day that you and I fail to take the enemy seriously, we lose the battle.

The Bible says that the devil is a real spiritual being—a "he." It never calls Satan an "it" or a "thing." The Bible also makes it clear that the devil has a heart, mind, will and personality. It talks about the devil's feelings, his thoughts and motives. All these are the attributes of a person. He is not a figment of your imagination or dark energy or evil "force." He is all evil and the real force of this world.

Now pay attention: Jesus Himself took Satan very seriously. He never made a joke about the devil or laughed about him the way the Church is doing today. Here are some of the titles Jesus used to describe the devil: a serpent, the prince of this world, the ruler of this world and the god of this world. Let's get something straight: Our Father, God almighty, owns everything, but Satan is the god of this world for a season. He is a master of manipulation. He manipulates science, education, politics, media, music, entertainment, etc. He does this for his own satisfaction.

Let's not stop there. Satan is also the real god whom the majority of the people on earth worship, whether they know it or not. This is a fact. Behind all religions other than Christianity, sorry to say, Satan is the one being worshiped. This is true even for many Christians who go to church on Sunday; you can tell the devil is their god by the way they live. This is because they love the things of this world rather than setting their minds and hearts on the things above, where Jesus Christ sits.

Check yourself: Who is your God? Remember one thing: There will always be a price to pay when the bill comes in. You might not be quite so happy in the end.

God asks Satan in the book of Job (I am paraphrasing it), "Where have you been?"

The devil replies, "I have been walking up and down the earth, watching over my real estate."

Now, let's get this clear and not get it twisted, not even for a second. This does not mean that God is helpless in this universe. No way!

God is allowing the devil, the prince of this world, to do his thing for a short season.

So why is God allowing this?

Well, let me ask you a question: Why is He allowing you to be you? Hello?

There are two things in this planet that rebel against God. They are the devil and humankind—that means us. And there is a thing called "free will." The Lord gives us the freedom to say yes or no to Him. The world uses that free will to go the wrong way. We blame God for everything, but no one is blaming the devil these days. What a joke! Let me just remind you that one thing the devil hates with everything he has is the book of Revelation, because it is over for him. The devil, his demons and kingdom are doomed. When you read through the book of Revelation, you come to the realization that the devil is nothing against God. He will be cast into the lake of fire.

I will leave you with this in mind: Jesus told us to pray every day against the devil. You know, that real prayer that He taught His disciples, when they said, "Lord, teach us to pray"?

Well, in case you forgot, He said to pray like this:

> Our Father in heaven,
> Hallowed be Your name.
> Your kingdom come.
> Your will be done
> On earth as it is in heaven.
> Give us this day our daily bread.
> And forgive us our debts,
> As we forgive our debtors.
> And do not lead us into temptation,
> But deliver us from the evil one.
> For Yours is the kingdom and the power and the
>   glory forever. Amen.
>
> Matthew 6:8–13 NKJV

When you pray, pray for

- the things that Jesus wants—His name, His will and His Kingdom;
- the things you need—vision, protection, your family, purpose and destiny; and
- forgiveness.

This is the key of this incredible prayer, so do not miss it. By praying "deliver us from the evil one," and praying it daily, you start your prayer by putting the Father first. End your prayer by finishing off the evil one, who is the devil. You will go on in victory and conquer your deliverance in Jesus' name. Amen.

5

Let the Battle Begin

This is a spiritual-warfare warning.

Before you step onto the battlefield and engage the enemy, you must first be secure in Christ Jesus. You must truly be born again and have accepted the finished work of the cross of Jesus Christ, through faith. He needs to be Lord and Savior of your life.

> You must believe that God came through the Person of Jesus Christ to the earth as a man.
>
> You must believe that He was crucified for your sins and my sins—the sins of the whole world.
>
> You must confess all your sins, whether they seem big or small. There is no justifying any sin. The precious blood of Jesus Christ, the Son of God, can set you free.
>
> You must know and confess that He was raised from the dead by the power of God.
>
> And you can bet your bottom dollar that He is coming back to establish His Kingdom on the earth.

Pray this with me so we are one hundred percent sure that you are ready for the battle:

Father, I come to You in the name of Jesus and confess all my sins before You. I ask for forgiveness of all my trespasses and iniquities that have been wrong before You. I bring myself to the foot of the cross and ask You to forgive me because I am a sinner. Please forgive me now, in Jesus' name.

Also repeat this:

Lord Jesus, I now believe that You are the Son of God and that You died on the wooden cross two thousand years ago for my sins. Wash my sins with Your own blood. I confess You as my Lord and Savior. Come into my life and dwell in my heart. Change me into the person You want me to be. I believe by faith that You have a plan and purpose for my life. I give You back the pen of my life so You can rewrite my story. I want to thank You with all my heart for coming into my life. In Jesus' name, amen.

Now the Battle Begins

Because you are a born-again believer, the prayers that come out of your mouth carry the authority of heaven. You now have all the angels and the arsenal of heaven on your side, ready to do battle to execute the judgments of God upon the devil and his kingdom. As a true follower of Jesus, the Son of God, you will be protected by the shadow of the almighty God. No evil spirits, no satanic attacks, no demonic arsenals will be able to prosper against you.

Declare and decree these Scriptures with me now:

If you openly declare that Jesus is Lord and believe in your heart that God raised him from the dead, you will be saved.

Romans 10:9 NLT

And they have defeated him by the blood of the Lamb and by their testimony. And they did not love their lives so much that they were afraid to die.

Revelation 12:11 NLT

My brother and sister, please listen to me very carefully. Before you step into the realm of the spirit through spiritual warfare, and against any demonic attack against you, there is something you must do: You must establish a foundation in Christ. If you have done this, then when the enemy attacks, the most he can accomplish is to shake you but not move you from the foundation upon which your feet have been planted by the Lord Jesus Christ.

Here is the enemy's game plan: If he can move you from the place where God has planted you, then he will delay your purpose and destiny. The enemy understands that he has no authority over the true believer, that he has no power. The only power he has is the power the believer renders to him. This is called giving the enemy legal rights to our lives. He then has the ability to entrap us and delay us spiritually.

The Bible says not to give ground or turf or a "foothold" to the enemy (Ephesians 4:27 NIV).

A Solid Foundation

Many Christians today do not have a foundation to stand on, or else they have cracks and leaks in their foundations. When the devil has hit you so hard and so violently that he has knocked you all the way back to the Flintstone era, and you find yourself living in Bedrock with Fred and Barney, you may be discouraged and dismayed and want to quit.

But remember what Scripture says:

> They are like trees planted along the riverbank, bearing fruit each season. Their leaves never wither, and they prosper in all they do.
>
> Psalm 1:3 NLT

> Finally, my brethren, be strong in the Lord and in the power of His might. Put on the whole armor of God, that you may be able to stand against the wiles of the devil. For we do not wrestle against flesh and blood, but against principalities, against powers, against the rulers of the darkness of this age, against spiritual hosts of wickedness in the heavenly places. Therefore take up the whole armor of God, that you may be able to withstand in the evil day, and having done all, to stand.
>
> Ephesians 6:10–13 NKJV

> Therefore we do not lose heart, but though our outer person is decaying, yet our inner person is being renewed day by day. For our momentary, light affliction is producing for us an eternal weight of glory far beyond all comparison, while we look not at the things which are seen, but at the things which are not seen; for the things which are seen are temporal, but the things which are not seen are eternal.
>
> 2 Corinthians 4:16–18 NASB

This is the true foundation that the Lord Jesus wants the believer to have against the enemy of our souls.

I want you to declare these things over your life today so we can build the foundation of spiritual warfare in your life, through Jesus Christ. Repeat these mighty declarations after me:

I declare and decree by faith in Jesus, the Son of God, that I stand in the power of God and trust in God. I believe that Jesus Christ is the Lord and King over my life. I believe in the power of the Holy Spirit who lives in me. I believe and trust in the unshakeable, all-powerful, unmovable Word of God. I trust and put my faith on the finished work of the cross and the blood of Jesus Christ, which will cover me, protect me and give me the victory. I stand on the truth of the Word of God. Jesus Christ offered His blood as a drink and His flesh as bread. The Bible says that whosoever eats this bread and drinks this blood proclaims His death until He comes again. Because of this promise, I am one with Him. I have eternal life, and I receive upon myself strength, power and might, and the anointing that comes through the blood of Jesus. I declare this over my life today, in Jesus' name.

Say these violent prayer points with me:

I cover myself with the blood of Jesus Christ, and let it resurrect in my life everything that is dead within me. I cover my mind, my eyes, my ears and my mouth with the blood of Jesus Christ. With the blood of Jesus Christ, I cover my home, my children, my family and all that I have right now, in Jesus' name. With the blood of Jesus, I cover my ministry, my purpose and destiny, my career, my finances, my marriage and my family in the name of Jesus Christ.

Let the all-powerful blood of Jesus Christ be a shield over me against the arsenals of the demonic world that are trying to come against me now. Father, let the blood of Your Son, Jesus Christ, make my home, my ministry, my purpose and my destiny be in stealth mode so that the satanic world and its radar system will not prosper against me and will all be destroyed in Jesus' name. I shake the devil's camp and confuse and smite them with the blood of Jesus Christ upon their heads now.

I release angels from Michael's quarters to go down and attack every evil force of darkness against me as I release the anointing and the fire of the Holy Spirit to do battle for me, in Jesus' name.

I declare and decree that the foundation I built today through these spiritual-warfare prayers will not be shaken, not be moved, not today, not tomorrow or ever in the name of Jesus Christ, my Lord and Savior.

Legal Rights, Strongholds and Bondages

Many of us experience powerful breakthrough and deliverance in our lives, but we fail to keep it. We will never conquer our deliverance if our spiritual foundation is not whole and complete through Christ Jesus, our Lord and Savior. That is why this chapter is so important in your life today.

As long as your foundation is weak, has cracks and is not built on the truth of the Word of God, the enemy will find ways to gain legal rights, strongholds and bondages. Even though we get delivered, many of us never conquer our deliverance and victory. As a devil worshiper, I was trained to attack Christians very differently from how I was trained to attack unbelievers. When I set my sights on attacking believers, my first assignment was to look at the foundation where the believer stood, which is called the "blueprint," to find any weaknesses or cracks in the foundation, and I would start my demonic attack from there.

I share this truth with you because I want God's best in your life. This is your brother, John Ramirez, speaking to you from the heart. I love you so much.

6

The Devil's Playbook

Let me share with you the strategies of the dark side and the tactics the enemy uses to entrap you, block you, delay you, confuse you and eventually destroy you.

I remember my life back in 2002 as if it were yesterday, when I lost my eyesight for three and a half months. I shared this in my testimony in chapter 2. What I did not tell you before was that I was under siege from the voice of the devil. His method of attack was to pound his voice in my ear and in my mind, and eventually in my heart, which is my will and emotions. He tried to break me down in the battlefield of my thoughts. The demonic blueprint he used in my head was his voice repeating over and over, day and night, "See, I can still get to you, and your God can't do anything about it. I still own you, and you can't leave me. I can still get to you whenever I want."

Those demonic words pounded in my head and in my spirit for three and a half months, day in and day out. This was his blueprint: to make me believe and come into agreement with him that I would never see my breakthrough, either in the attack or in the physical battle I was enduring.

One of the enemy's blueprints for our lives has to do with timing; he finds you at the most vulnerable moment in your walk with the Lord. That is part of the blueprint he uses upon believers today.

He did it to Jesus.

Then Jesus was led by the Spirit into the wilderness to be tempted by the devil. After fasting forty days and forty nights, he was hungry. The tempter came to him and said, "If you are the Son of God, tell these stones to become bread."

Jesus answered, "It is written: 'Man shall not live on bread alone, but on every word that comes from the mouth of God.'"

Then the devil took him to the holy city and had him stand on the highest point of the temple. "If you are the Son of God," he said, "throw yourself down. For it is written: 'He will command his angels concerning you, and they will lift you up in their hands, so that you will not strike your foot against a stone.'"

Jesus answered him, "It is also written: 'Do not put the Lord your God to the test.'"

Again, the devil took him to a very high mountain and showed him all the kingdoms of the world and their splendor. "All this I will give you," he said, "if you will bow down and worship me."

Jesus said to him, "Away from me, Satan! For it is written: 'Worship the Lord your God, and serve him only.'"

Then the devil left him, and angels came and attended him.

Matthew 4:1–11 NIV

See how the enemy used three different strategies of attack? The first was when the devil tried to tempt Jesus to do something out of the will of God, as Satan does to us many times. The second was when he tempted Jesus to tempt the Father. Many times, we tempt Jesus by listening to the devil when he says, "If Jesus loves you, why are you going through this? If you are a real Christian, why are you struggling?" The devil's blueprint is for you to question God and His authority.

In the third strategy, Satan showed Jesus the kingdoms of the world, which meant the lust of the eyes and the heart. He was showing Jesus the blueprints of the world. In other words, he was saying that Jesus could take a shortcut and have all of this before the right time. How many times does the enemy tempt us with things that look good, and we take the bait, thinking that the Lord is blessing us? But in reality we forfeit our true blessings because we go ahead of God's timing and His perfect will for our lives. We do not wait on Him, and we never get our true breakthrough because we settle for a counterfeit blessing.

The Word says this: "The seventh angel sounded his trumpet, and there were loud voices in heaven, which said: 'The kingdom of the world has become the kingdom of our Lord and of his Messiah, and he will reign for ever and ever'" (Revelation 11:15 NIV).

The Devil's Game

As you can see, Scripture itself says that if Jesus had taken the bait earlier, He would have missed out on the blessing of the Father. The devil knows how to play a good game. He is after one thing: He wants from you what he will never have, and that is *breakthrough*. The devil will never have his own breakthrough in his existence. The Bible says that we move from glory to glory, from breakthrough to breakthrough, from victory to victory.

The enemy knows that a believer who is walking in the purpose and perfect will of Jesus Christ will become a spiritual corpse if there are no breakthroughs in his or her life. The devil understands the blueprint of *your* life. It is time you understand the blueprint of his demonic kingdom.

Satan implants negative thoughts to create strongholds that incarcerate your mind. He builds walls in your mind through bondages to the things you have suffered in the past—hurts, betrayals and wounds that never close—and he uses these against you. This animal called the devil has demonic agents sent to search out the blueprints of your life and your walk with Jesus Christ. The purpose is to create strongholds and bondages in two areas. The first is through generational curses, whether they be sickness, alcohol, mental illness, homosexuality, depression, oppression, molestation—any generational scars in your family. The second area of bondage is that which you create of your own free will, such as pornography, lust of the eyes, gossip spirits and any other dead words or conversations that have come out of your mouth.

Proverbs 18:21 (NIV) says, "The tongue has the power of life and death, and those who love it will eat its fruit."

Hear me again: The devil chases one thing and one thing only in the life of every believer, and that word is *breakthrough*. I will repeat it again: *breakthrough*. You need insight into the devil's kingdom, his wiles and schemes, ways he operates and moves in the spirit realm, his demonic thinking. You need to understand the arsenals and strategies he is trying to use to sink the believer; we cannot defeat what we do not understand.

Does the devil own the blueprint of your spiritual life? Has the devil incarcerated your breakthrough? If he did incarcerate your breakthrough, then he owns the blueprint of your life. Be honest with yourself. When was the last time you experienced moving from glory to glory?

Do you find yourself stuck in the same condition year in and year out? Are there empty things in your life that you repeat over and over? Have you taken one step forward only to be knocked back three steps? Are you on the edge of your breakthrough and something always seems to happen? Many of God's people are under siege at this moment because the enemy owns legal rights to the blueprints of their callings, purpose and destiny.

It is time to break free. If this devil brings frustration every time you get to the end of your promised land, no matter how hard you try to cross over, if there is always a spiritual roadblock to stop your blessing when your breakthrough is staring you in the face from the other side, if your blessing is so close yet so far—then it is time to fight back and strip the devil's hands of your blueprint. It is time to cancel his assignment that is stealing your breakthrough. As you release these prayers into the spirit realm, the power of the Holy Spirit will break and destroy the devil's agenda against you, and every satanic demon of breakthrough will shrivel up and die.

Declarations for Breakthrough

Repeat these words after me. Lock in your faith as you say them out loud:

Every enemy that is trying to occupy my promised land, be evicted in the name of Jesus.

Every satanic attack against the blueprint of my purpose and destiny be destroyed by the fire of the Holy Spirit, in Jesus' name.

Father, I ask You to send an ambush against every devil that is trying to steal my breakthrough.

Lord, let the fire of the Holy Spirit blow against every devil that is sitting on my breakthrough, in the name of Jesus.

Lord, break through the front line of my enemies and remove every demonic spirit that is trying to rob my breakthrough.

Father, let every demonic devil that is blocking my ministry be destroyed by the fire of the Holy Spirit.

Every devil that is blocking my breakthrough, I put the judgments of God upon your head, in Jesus' name.

Every sorcerer, witch and warlock that is trying to shut down my destiny and purpose, that has infiltrated the blueprint of my life, let the fire of God destroy you now, in Jesus' name.

Father, in Jesus' name, let the fire of God fall upon every wicked demon that seeks my destruction, in Jesus' name.

Every demon that is trying to destroy my blessing, I chop your head off, in the name of Jesus.

These prayers are sealed and covered in the blood of our Lord Jesus Christ. Read this Scripture:

> "Now I say to you that you are Peter (which means 'rock'), and upon this rock I will build my church, and all the powers of hell will not conquer it."
>
> Matthew 16:18 NLT

Now take out the name *Peter* and put your name there. Then say,

Devil, listen to me, I am not done with you yet. I have just started to attack your kingdom, in Jesus' name.

One thing I want to share quickly is that our victory is not won while we are on defense. To possess and destroy the gates of the enemy, we must go on the offense against the gates of hell. You are the child of God and have all the arsenals of heaven at your disposal. It is time to aim that ammunition at the devil and his cronies, and get on the offense.

Repeat these prayers with me now:

I receive the anointing of a warrior of spiritual-warfare fighter, in the name of Jesus.

Let every gate of my enemy be destroyed by fire, in Jesus' name.

Let every roadblock of the enemy shrivel up and die, in Jesus' name.

Let the thunder and fire of God fall upon every demon's head that has been assigned to destroy the blueprint of my life, in Jesus' name.

I arrest the gatekeepers that are standing in position to block my breakthrough, in Jesus' name.

I pull down every stronghold and bondage that the enemy has sent against me, in Jesus' name.

I destroy and dismantle every roadblock in my mind, in the name of Jesus.

Every problem, roadblock, distraction and hindrance that has my name on it, die now, in Jesus' name.

I renounce Satan and his kingdom, and I acknowledge that they are my enemies, in Jesus' name.

I exercise my authority over every entrapment the enemy has set against me and my family, in Jesus' name.

I seal all my prayers as I decree and declare them over my life and over my purpose and destiny today, in the name of Jesus.

Declarations for Blessing

Declare and decree these blessings after me:

I release the blessings of the Kingdom of heaven over me now, in Jesus' name.

I decree and declare that I will walk in the fullness of my purpose and destiny, in Jesus' name. This is sealed in the blood of Jesus Christ.

I release the anointing of the Holy Spirit upon my life now, in the name of Jesus.

I command everything that has been lost or stolen to come back and be made manifest now, in the name of Jesus.

I release the fullness of what God has for me and my family now, in Jesus' name.

I declare and decree that I will live in complete healing, health, wholeness and the abundant blessings of heaven all the days of my life, in Jesus' name.

I speak resurrection power over every area of my life that needs to be resurrected, in Jesus' name.

I speak life and not death to every area of my life and my family's life, in Jesus' name.

I cover the blueprint of my life, my family, my ministry, my marriage and my children in the blood of Jesus Christ.

Take a moment now to praise the Lord Jesus for your deliverance and for receiving your breakthrough, in Jesus' name.

7

Setups from the Enemy

The enemy has setups, but we have God's Word and His promises and principles to fight the good fight of faith. Many times, in my travels and in the opportunities God has given me, I have been fortunate to do hundreds of altar calls as well as spiritual-warfare boot camps where people share their hearts with me. Many precious brothers and sisters ask the million-dollar question: How do I overcome the dark places of my life? Some people suppress it, and others choose to put a hallelujah on it. Many other Christians ignore it and pretend they are fine. None of these responses is spiritually healthy. I will help you and prepare you to face the enemy head on.

Many of us have the mentality of a Moses generation; that generation died in the desert and never made it to the Promised Land. God has called us to come out of the desert into our purpose and destiny. It is time to be the Joshuas that God has called us to be and to confront the enemy on his turf. The devil is occupying your promised land and standing in the place where you are supposed to be standing, not him.

God's Word says, "Be strong and very courageous. Be careful to obey all the law my servant Moses gave you; do not turn from it to the right or to the left, that you may be successful wherever you go" (Joshua 1:7 NIV).

It is time to face the enemy that is occupying the territory God has promised you. Why are we acting like the spies who went out and came back with a bad report? We need to be like Joshua and Caleb—of a different spirit—for the times that we are living in today. We are living as if we have no authority in Christ, yet look at the position of true disciples:

> The seventy-two returned with joy and said, "Lord, even the demons submit to us in your name."
>
> He replied, "I saw Satan fall like lightning from heaven. I have given you authority to trample on snakes and scorpions and to overcome all the power of the enemy; nothing will harm you."
>
> Luke 10: 17–19 NIV

Jesus did not stop there; He also blessed us: "When Jesus had called the Twelve together, he gave them power and authority to drive out all demons and to cure diseases" (Luke 9:1 NIV).

I am going to hit you with another Scripture:

> "And these signs will accompany those who believe: In my name they will drive out demons; they will speak in new tongues; they will pick up snakes with their hands; and when they drink deadly poison, it will not hurt them at all; they will place their hands on sick people, and they will get well."
>
> Mark 16:17–18 NIV

Why are we hiding from God the way Adam and Eve did? It is because we believe that the condition the devil has put us in is a permanent place.

God is saying to you, *Where are you today?*

It is time to come out of your fig leaf of fear, torment, deception, suppression and depression. It is time to come out of the dark places of your life, out of the unhealthy conditions of every infirmity spirit that has attacked you. It is time to defeat every tormenting devil that torments your mind, your thoughts, your thinking. Do you not know that the devil has been defeated even though he is putting up a fight?

> Then war broke out in heaven. Michael and his angels fought against the dragon, and the dragon and his angels fought back. But he was not strong enough, and they lost their place in heaven. The great dragon was hurled down—that ancient serpent called the devil, or Satan, who leads the whole world astray. He was hurled to the earth, and his angels with him.
>
> Then I heard a loud voice in heaven say: "Now have come the salvation and the power and the kingdom of our God, and the authority of his Messiah. For the accuser of our brothers and sisters, who accuses them before our God day and night, has been hurled down. They triumphed over him by the blood of the Lamb and by the word of their testimony."
>
> Revelation 12:7–11 NIV

Serve the Devil an Eviction Notice

Dear saint, where is your boldness and authority? Rise up from the ashes of your life, put on the Holy Spirit and look the devil in the eye. Then say, without your voice quavering, "You picked the wrong Christian to mess with."

Ask yourself, who sets the battle plan? Who has the authority to pull down strongholds? Who should lead the warfare? Let me share a thought with you before we beat the devil down like a piñata at a party.

Here is a quick insight as to what the Bible says about pulling down strongholds: "The weapons we fight with are not the weapons of the world. On the contrary, they have divine power to demolish strongholds" (2 Corinthians 10:4 NIV). We begin this spiritual warfare by binding the strongman: "How can anyone enter a strong man's house and carry off his possessions unless he first ties up the strong man? Then he can plunder his house" (Matthew 12:29 NIV).

Binding is a spiritual-warfare weapon that God has given us to paralyze the devil and his attacks and immobilize him from accomplishing his mission. I want to say one thing, that whatever Satan has bound needs to be loosed today.

Remember the woman in the Bible whom Satan had bound with a spirit of infirmity for eighteen years (see Luke 13:10–17)? Now go to Luke 17:11–17 (NIV):

> Now on his way to Jerusalem, Jesus traveled along the border between Samaria and Galilee. As he was going into a village, ten men who had leprosy met him. They stood at a distance and called out in a loud voice, "Jesus, Master, have pity on us!"
>
> When he saw them, he said, "Go, show yourselves to the priests." And as they went, they were cleansed.
>
> One of them, when he saw he was healed, came back, praising God in a loud voice. He threw himself at Jesus' feet and thanked him—and he was a Samaritan.
>
> Jesus asked, "Were not all ten cleansed? Where are the other nine?"

Who has the authority to pull down strongholds and break bondages and bind the strongman? Who should lead the spiritual warfare in the battle today? "Jesus called his twelve disciples to him and gave them authority to drive out impure spirits and to heal every disease and sickness" (Matthew 10:1 NIV).

And read these words again: "I have given you authority to trample on snakes and scorpions and to overcome all the power of the enemy; nothing will harm you" (Luke 10:19 NIV).

What is the calling and mandate of the Church? "And these signs will accompany those who believe: In my name they will drive out demons; they will speak in new tongues" (Mark 16:17 NIV).

And what is the job of the Church? "I will give you the keys of the kingdom of heaven; whatever you bind on earth will be bound in heaven, and whatever you loose on earth will be loosed in heaven" (Matthew 16:19 NIV).

The Church of Jesus Christ has to put the devil in his place.

But before you do, you must become spiritually clean before the throne room of God; this is a requirement before you can conquer your deliverance.

Prayer of Confession and Repentance

A prayer of repentance is very powerful because it puts you in a place of mercy and grace with God. When you are forgiven, the devil is stripped of his powers over you and your life, and every satanic control he has over you is broken. We must confess and repent of our sins. The devil hates repentance. Repentance destroys the legal rights and grounds that the devil and his demons hold over you.

These prayers are very powerful, so repeat them after me:

Holy Spirit, I present my spirit, soul and body to You now in the unmatchable name of Jesus Christ.

Holy Spirit, I ask You to help me uncover the sins I have committed, known and unknown, in the name of Jesus.

I come to the throne of mercy and repent of all my sins, in the name of Jesus.

71

I confess and repent of all sins of my heart, my mouth and my mind, in the name of Jesus.

Lord, forgive me for all my sins that have offended You, known and unknown, in Jesus' name.

Holy Spirit, please forgive me if I ever grieved You in any way, in Jesus' name.

Holy Spirit, I ask You in the name of Jesus to create in me a new heart and a new mind that desires the full obedience of Jesus in my life.

Prayer to Remove Satan's Legal Grounds

There are some things we should not be allowing in our lives. The Bible says that "the thief comes only to steal and kill and destroy; [but Jesus] came so that [we might] have life, and have it more abundantly" (John 10:10 NASB).

Satan's mission is to bind, restrict and arrest you, and frustrate you out of your purpose and destiny, but he can succeed only if he has legal rights and grounds to operate on. Remember that legal grounds are given through spiritual doors, gateways and portals that we open through sin and disobedience. Legal grounds are also given to Satan through the sins of our ancestors. I believe in my heart that a lot of our struggles that we face (whether spiritually or physically) are because many times we are victims of generational curses that we inherit from either our father's or mother's side, or the generations before.

It can be an alcohol issue, it can be an infirmity, it can be a witchcraft curse if someone in the family got involved in the occult, and now we are paying the consequences spiritually and physically from a door that was opened either unconsciously or consciously—and now you are fighting these demons.

If not dealt with, curses from those sins can trace down our family trees, through our family bloodlines, even from all the way back to Adam and Eve.

We need to make up our minds and come into agreement with God because, as I said before, the battlefield starts in our minds. The devil's number-one trick is to put a spirit of manipulation in your mind to control and dominate your thoughts, speech, heart, emotions and will. It is time to renounce and disown the basis for these legal rights in every demonic circumstance that has us bound.

As we pray these powerful arsenal prayers below, you will cancel, revoke and remove every legal ground and right the enemy has accomplished over your life. Let's get violent on the devil now:

I renounce all agreements I have made with Satan and his demons, in the name of Jesus.

I renounce and reject all satanic offerings made to me by the devil and his agents, in Jesus' name.

I renounce all lust, perversion and immorality spirits. Come out now, in the name of Jesus.

I renounce and break away all witchcraft, sorcery and divination, and every level of the occult affecting me in the past and present, in the name of Jesus.

I renounce every ungodly soul tie, and every satanic and immoral relationship, in the name of Jesus.

I renounce all hatred, anger, resentment, revenge, retaliation, unforgiveness and bitterness, in the name of Jesus.

This year, right now, I renounce pride, every jealousy and every ungodly covenant, in the name of Jesus.

I renounce fear and every tormenting devil, and every negative thought that has been tormenting me, in the name of Jesus.

I renounce every ungodly covenant, oath and vow I have made with my mouth, in the name of Jesus.
Satan, listen to me, I renounce you, in the name of Jesus.
Satan, the Lord rebukes you. I will receive my deliverance now, in the name of Jesus.

Say this now to remove unbelief from your heart:

I receive my deliverance now, in the name of Jesus, and I will maintain my deliverance until Jesus calls me home, by the power of the Holy Spirit, which will cover me, in Jesus' name.

I want to add a quick word to encourage every Christian who has been called to get involved with spiritual warfare. Unfold your hands and take up your weapons so that you do not become a casualty in the battlefield. You can be victorious and more than a conqueror. You can make Jesus Christ proud that He picked you for the ultimate spiritual battle of this lifetime.

8

The Elephant in the Room

Like the proverbial elephant in the room, the Church does not talk about the condition of the Body of Christ. They do not address it, but I do. I see it on the front lines everywhere I go.

Remember when Jesus went to the pool of Bethesda and saw the colony of sick people? This was a colony of people who were sick spiritually and physically. Jesus showed up there and ministered to them. Don't miss this: Jesus *went* to the colony of sick people and sought them out. So why are we not showing up at the battlefields and picking up our brothers and sisters who are wounded?

One day as a young believer, I was invited to minister at a hospital for children with terminal illnesses and deformities whose parents had abandoned them there and never came back because of their shame. The parents were embarrassed to have them as part of their families.

Other people were at the mall that day, looking for Jesus in the gifts and decorations of the Christmas season, and I am sure that the mall was filled with Christmas cheer. But the same

Jesus who was at the Pool of Bethesda was not at the mall that day; He was at the hospital. He was there as my brothers and I sang our hearts out with Christmas carols and put big smiles on the faces of those beautiful children.

The Fragmented Body–the Church

The reason we have the elephant in the room and no one wants to talk about it is because the Church is a type of Samson, who was beguiled by Delilah. I have heard my friend Pastor Bill from First Love Ministries in Kansas City make this comparison in his profound way: "The Church is a type of Samson, lying in the lap of Delilah, which is a type of the world."

We know the story of Samson, a man called by God from his mother's womb. He was separated for a special calling and anointed by God to fulfill a divine plan. That is the story of many of us today. We were handpicked by the Lord Jesus Christ before the foundations of the world, preordained, and later set apart by the finished work of the cross and salvation through Christ Jesus. It is sad to say that many of us come into salvation—the best thing that could ever happen to anyone on this planet—but we never complete the work we are called to do because we never come into the fullness of our salvation. We never enter into the promised land of our purpose and destiny. In short, we fail to align ourselves with the will of God.

I say with a broken heart that the Church has become like Samson.

John, what do you mean by that?

I mean that there is no spiritual growth, no spiritual maturity, no spiritual strength through the Holy Spirit, and the faith we do have is anemic. We have no spiritual endurance to fight the good fight—just like Samson at the end of his days.

Physically blinded and tied between two pillars of a pagan temple, he stands as a metaphor for many of us today: tied up in bondage and strongholds and spiritually blinded. Some of us experience a degree of deliverance, but few conquer their deliverance.

And this is because, as Pastor Bill says, the Church, like Samson, is sleeping in the lap of Delilah. In other words, the Church has a form of godliness but denies the power we have to set us free. Back in my day, we had an old saying: "The proof is in the pudding." I write this chapter from a broken heart as I reflect on the hundreds of prayer requests I receive through my ministry from loving brothers and sisters. Without a doubt, I know they love Jesus Christ, but this is the condition they are in because of the condition of the Church. This is their story. Yet I know in my heart that it is not the end of their story.

Or yours.

I declare God's Word over you:

> Christ redeemed us from the curse of the law by becoming a curse for us, for it is written: "Cursed is everyone who is hung on a pole." He redeemed us in order that the blessing given to Abraham might come to the Gentiles through Christ Jesus, so that by faith we might receive the promise of the Spirit.
>
> Galatians 3:13–14 NIV

> And the Lord shall deliver me from every evil work, and will preserve me unto his heavenly kingdom: to whom be glory for ever and ever. Amen.
>
> 2 Timothy 4:18 KJV

Below are some of the prayer requests from my precious brothers and sisters around the world, whom I love dearly. Many times, in our prayer closet, we do not aim spiritual-warfare arsenals in the right direction to bring down the spiritual targets that are against us. These arsenal prayers are great examples of how to use our spiritual-warfare weapons in the right way.

Prayer Request

"I ask for prayer over my life, my marriage and my kids. I don't want the devil to control my life any longer. I will no longer allow the enemy to keep me on the ground. I want to break the curses and generational curses as well. Please pray for my spiritual life and for my husband so that he will repent and come to God."

ARSENAL PRAYER

Father, in Jesus' name, we break and destroy every hindrance, delay, blockage and distraction against my sister, her marriage and her family, in Jesus' name.

Prayer Request

"I need prayers, here in the city of São Paulo, Brazil, for my husband to get out of drugs and other situations and come back to the Lord. I've been watching your videos and prayers, and they are helping me keep going. I am so tired of it and, I'm sorry, many times I want to quit. Please help me with your prayers. Thank you so much."

ARSENAL PRAYER

Father, in Jesus' name, we destroy every spirit of addiction upon this husband, we rebuke every backsliding spirit against him, we call the prodigal home now into the arms of Jesus. And we pray for my sister to be refreshed in the Spirit, in Jesus' name.

Prayer Request

"I'm physically possessed 24/7 by witchcraft or something else unseen and now unheard. I need this to stop because this is affecting my mind and memory now. I'm constantly being coerced physically to say no whenever I just try to move my body around, or try to do anything. I thought God has dominion over all this stuff! Please help me!"

ARSENAL PRAYER

Father, right now, in the name of Jesus, I bind every satanic devil and every witchcraft spirit that is attacking this person. I put the judgments of God upon every wicked demon to leave this person now, in the name of Jesus.

Prayer Request

"I received deliverance a couple of days ago. I'm just wanting to make sure the demons are gone. Where I live there aren't good churches that are actually awake. My son has been wrapped up in addiction for about sixteen years. He has been in and out of prison and now has two children. He is actively using. Just listening to Brother Ramirez's messages made me realize that my son is in a spiritual war. Please pray with me for complete deliverance of my son and a return to worshiping Jesus Christ."

ARSENAL PRAYER

Father, I touch and agree with my precious sister right now, and I break off her every spirit of retaliation, revenge and retribution against her. I destroy them by the blood of Jesus. I pray for her son and destroy every devil of addiction and pharmakeia related to every drug that has entered his body. I command it to come out now, in the name of Jesus. I declare the salvation of Jesus Christ upon his life right now. In Jesus' name, Amen.

Prayer Request

"Pray that my faith will not fail and pray for my heart and that all disobedience breaks in my life. I repent from all my sins."

ARSENAL PRAYER

Today, in the name of Jesus, I curse to the root every spirit of unbelief off my sister right now, and I declare her faith to increase now, in Jesus' name. Amen.

Prayer Request

"Please pray that God will loose these demonic bindings and lift this oppression from me and my family and shut down these demonic attacks. And bless and grow my ministry and send me help. I appreciate you following the call on your life."

ARSENAL PRAYER

Today in the name of Jesus Christ, devil, we put you on notice: Release my sister now. I command every spirit of oppression and depression and discouragement to leave her now. I break every demonic attack over her purpose and destiny, over her life, right now, in Jesus' name.

Prayer Request

"I have had a lifetime of anxiety, panic attacks and thoughts of death, very dark, tormenting thoughts. I've taken meds for the panic disorder for years, but I truly want to be free, once and for all. I have had prayer and gone through deliverance several times, yet I am still having to cast down the same thoughts. These thoughts scare me at times. Just recently I started reading your books and speaking those prayers every day in addition to my own time in the Word, and it seems as though the heat has been turned up. I am hungry for my freedom, and I have been seeking God for two years about this. Am I doing anything wrong? I have forgiven and confessed to everything. I know for a fact that medication only sedates you; it doesn't deal with anything. Please help."

ARSENAL PRAYER

Decree and declare this right now over your life:
"Devil, listen to me, enough is enough. Today is my day for complete deliverance and victory. I come against every spirit of anxiety, every spirit of death and premature death, panic attack, every generational curse and every devil that is trying to afflict my body and control it, and I curse it to the root. Let it shrivel up and die, in Jesus' name, and never return."

Prayer Request

"Can I schedule a deliverance session with John? Or can I go to where he is preaching and do the altar call? I have voodoo and Santeria spirits from my past, prior to being saved, harassing me, and I really need a deliverance minister who can stop them from trying to oppress me."

ARSENAL PRAYER

Father, right now in the name of Jesus, I bind and destroy every harassing devil that is afflicting my sister right now, and I destroy every Santeria and voodoo contract and legal right against her with the blood of Jesus. In Jesus' name, Amen.

Prayer Request

"I am a sixty-three-year-old man, a believer in Jesus for forty-five years, born with cerebral palsy and profound hearing loss. I am asking for healing from lateral scoliosis, brain atrophy, mild cognitive impairment, mild vertigo, hearing loss and, finally, cerebral palsy. Thank you!"

ARSENAL PRAYER

I bind the strongman named the spirit of infirmity in the name of Jesus Christ. We destroy and dismantle every satanic and demonic attack of sickness, now in the name of Jesus. I declare and decree over your life Psalm 103:1–3 (NIV): "Praise the LORD, my soul; all my inmost being, praise his holy name. Praise the LORD, my soul, and forget not all his benefits—who forgives all your sins and heals all your diseases."

Prayer Request

"I ask prayer for deliverance for homosexual, lesbian and transgender feelings. Just recently in August I was attacked with these feelings all over again and sinned against God. I don't want these feelings and feelings for that person. I also feel oppression in my mind. Please help me; I'm desperate. Thank you."

ARSENAL PRAYER

Today we give the devil an eviction notice. We destroy all patterns and cycles of repeat against you. We uproot the spirit of homosexuality that is against you. I come against all rejection, self-condemnation, fear, shame, guilt and any molestation spirits. Let them be destroyed by Jesus Christ and the finished work of the cross. I declare and decree that whom the Son sets free is free indeed (that means you!). I declare Psalm 91 over your life in the untouchable name of Jesus Christ. Be free.

Prayer Request

"Please pray for my friend to be delivered, healed and set free from drug addiction, an abusive boyfriend, alcoholism and suicidal and self-hurting behaviors like cutting."

ARSENAL PRAYER

Father, right now we bind the spirit of self-infliction against this precious one. We bind the spirit of alcoholism, pharmakeia spirit, spirits of death and suicide, self-hatred, every mind-controlling spirit, come out of your mind. All trauma and rejection spirits of every kind, come out now, in Jesus' name. I declare and decree over your life that you will live and not die, and you are healed and set free by the power of the Holy Spirit now, in Jesus' name.

Prayer Request

"I have multiple people using witchcraft on me. Please help me to pray for the witchcraft to stop and to bring these people to Christ. Also, the stress is giving me heart palpitations. Please pray to stop these, too. Thank you!"

ARSENAL PRAYER

Right now we bind, rebuke and break the spirits of witchcraft, voodoo, hexes and vexes that are against you, in the name of Jesus. We curse to the root the spirit of infirmity through witchcraft right now, in the name of Jesus. We call these people from the darkness and into the light of salvation of Jesus Christ right now.

Repeat after me: "I declare and decree that I loose myself from every spirit of witchcraft against me and take authority over every spell and every plot of the enemy against me, in the name of Jesus. I command all demons associated through witchcraft to leave me now and never return."

Prayer Request

"Please pray for my son to reunite with God, his family and friends. Three and a half years ago, he got married on Halloween night. No one was invited. He slowly drifted away from God, family and friends. Two and a half years ago, he disowned me, his mother. He was thirty-four years old when he said that. We were a very close, loving family. He always used to say I was the best mother he could ever ask for. He was also a born-again Christian and was very involved in the church. Everyone wondered what happened to him. Please pray for him to reunite with family and God."

ARSENAL PRAYER

Declare this confession over your life and your loved one:
"The Bible says, 'See, I have this day set you over the nations and over the kingdoms, to root out and to pull down, to destroy and to throw down, to build and to plant'" (*Jeremiah* 1:10 NKJV).

"I lay the ax of the Holy Spirit to the root of every witchcraft attack against me in the name of Jesus. I command all ungodly soul ties to be uprooted, in the name

of Jesus. Every demonic root planted in my dreams, die now, in the name of Jesus. Every root planted in my mind, die, in the name of Jesus. I curse to the root every satanic wedding, in the name of Jesus. I break and destroy the covenant of witchcraft that I made, in the name of Jesus. Father God, let your holy fire destroy every demonic alignment that I made in my life. Let them be destroyed by the fire of Your Holy Spirit. I call back my prodigal son, right now, in the name of Jesus. I destroy all division and discord in my family and release unity, restoration and healing, in the untouchable name of Jesus Christ."

Destroying the Tormenters

These are the fragmented places that our precious brothers and sisters in the Church live. Today they will all be canceled by the power of the Holy Spirit in the name of Jesus.

Beloved one, the Bible tells us that the enemy comes to kill, steal and destroy. Today we are very aware that Satan has unleashed the most satanic, dangerous soldiers from his kingdom to cause major damage to the Body of Christ. It is sad to say that he has been very effective against God's people. But I have Good News. The Bible says that Jesus overcame the world, so fear not.

Here are some arsenal prayers that will cancel the satanic attacks.

I bind all wickedness in high places and every evil throne of the enemy that is against me, my family, my ministry, my purpose and my destiny. I destroy them now, in the name of Jesus.

I bind all evil dominions and strongmen of lack, poverty, unemployment, misery and sickness against my life, family and loved ones. Let them shrivel up and die, in Jesus' name.

I bind every witchcraft control and mind-binding spirit, in the name of Jesus. I strip each spirit of the power and rank that is given to it, and the assignment and authority over my life and family, purpose and destiny, in Jesus' name.

I command every witchcraft and satanic arrow to depart from me, my head, body, spirit and soul. Every astral-projecting devil, I destroy the silver cord that is trying to come into my home, family and ministry. I release the fire of the Holy Spirit upon every witch and warlock, in Jesus' name.

Let every satanic meeting and gathering against me be destroyed, in the name of Jesus.

Father, I thank You that You are my shield and protector—for me, my family, my ministry, my purpose and my destiny.

9

Encountering the Real Jesus

Today many of us find ourselves walking with God and using Jesus' name in a thousand ways, rebuking or binding the enemy, or loosing the favor of God upon our lives. These all sound very good, and we may have the right intention, but the reality is that there is no power and no anointing behind it.

Many of us sound like the sons of Sceva because we do not have a real, deep relationship with Jesus. It is like having a plane sitting on the runway; it can take you anywhere and everywhere, but if there is no pilot, your plane is not going anywhere. Or it is like a car that goes from zero to sixty miles per hour in two seconds, but you do not have keys to the vehicle. Many of us as Christians have the Christian talk, the Christian jargon, but no deep relationship with the Holy Spirit.

Jesus said this: "Nevertheless I tell you the truth; it is expedient for you that I go away: for if I go not away, the Comforter will not come unto you; but if I depart, I will send him unto you" (John 16:7 KJV).

The Father promises us the Holy Spirit so He can take us into a deeper relationship with Jesus Christ—not into religion or a list of rules or a format. Only the Holy Spirit will bring you deeper with Jesus and reveal the love that the Father has for you. Are you ready to grow in intimacy with the Holy Spirit? It is the Holy Spirit—the third Person of the Trinity—who equips and empowers us, guides us and strengthens us for the battles we will face, both the ones of today and the ones of tomorrow.

Selah. Stop and meditate or reflect on this.

Everywhere I go, I hear people say "I know God" or "Do you know God?" It has become a Christian cliché. To *know* God is to honor and serve Him. Jesus always mentioned the Father in everything He did. Jesus knew the hearts of the masses that followed Him, and He would say, "You want to be with Me because I fed you, not because you understood the miracles." In the gospel of John, for instance, He said this: "Most assuredly, I say to you, you seek Me, not because you saw the signs, but because you ate of the loaves and were filled" (John 6:26 NKJV).

Why did Jesus refer to the signs and miracles? Because they pointed to the Father. It is like being on a road trip and seeing a sign that reads "70 miles to NYC." We know we are not in New York City, but we are on our way. The same goes for the way Jesus led the disciples and those He fed. It was not about the loaf of bread and fishes; that was not the main point. He was revealing the love of the Father—namely that He is loving and cares for us.

Yet we struggle with that today. Let's be honest. In the world we live in, many of us grew up without a natural dad. Unfortunately, we miss God's best in our lives because we celebrate the signs, wonders and miracles, but we leave the Father, Son and Holy Spirit out of it.

We see our provision, we see our breakthrough, we see our miracles. And it becomes just lusting after things and wanting things, but no desire for a deep, ongoing, long-term relationship with the Father and Son, through the power of the Holy

Spirit. We need to see the faithfulness and compassion of Jesus Christ's miracles with evidence of the Father's mercy, grace and love toward us.

The Give-Me Mentality

It is time to reprogram our minds. We have drifted into a bless-me mentality, but for me the true blessing that I want in my life is not the material but the love of the Father, who loves me though His Son Jesus Christ. We need to grow into a deeper maturity and understanding of who He is. When that happens, then you will know who you are in Christ.

I am sick and tired of being sick and tired of fake Christianity, and I hope you feel the same. It always leaves you on the surface and in the shallow waters of who Christ really is in your life and mine. Paul says in Ephesians 1:3 (NKJV), "Blessed be the God and Father of our Lord Jesus Christ, who has blessed us with every spiritual blessing in the heavenly places in Christ." What an incredible promise for God's people today!

These promises become mere words if we do not know what these spiritual blessings are. How can we enjoy the blessings God has promised us if we cannot comprehend them? It is sad to say that many churches today do not even offer discipleship classes anymore. So how do I know what being in Christ is really all about? That is one of the reasons the devil is having a field day with the Church at large. If you are not rooted and grounded, the devil can move you and shake you and do whatever he wants with you.

Selah. Stop and meditate.

We come to the cross of Jesus Christ and understand: "For God so loved the world that He gave His only begotten Son, that whoever believes in Him should not perish but have everlasting life" (John 3:16 NKJV).

89

And in Ephesians 1:18–20 (NKJV) we read: "That you may know . . . what is the exceeding greatness of His power toward us who believe, according to the working of His mighty power which He worked in Christ when He raised Him from the dead and seated Him at His right hand in the heavenly places."

We read these Scriptures but do not understand them spiritually. Let's be honest and transparent: Many are forgiven, cleansed and redeemed but still live miserable lives. Many are forgiven, cleansed and redeemed but continue to go from peaks to valleys. They never have a sense of being fulfilled in Christ, yo-yoing from spiritual highs to depressing lows. How can this be? Let me tell you why: Because we never get past the crucifixion of our Savior, and so we miss the power of the resurrection. Then we miss it all.

Christ is seated at the right hand of the Father; therefore, if we are in Christ we are actually seated with Jesus. What I can see in my heart and the spirit realm is that many of those seats are empty because we never reach that place. This is what Paul refers to in Ephesians 2:6 (NKJV): "[God] raised us up together, and made us sit together in the heavenly places in Christ Jesus."

But know this: The Law also abides in you and me. He has made us His Temple on the earth, His dwelling place. You are the Temple. The seat of your heart . . . Is He really there, or is the seat empty?

Selah. Stop and meditate.

Beloved one, it is time to lay down your doubts and fears.

Seeing Jesus in the Storm

One day during His time on earth Jesus did something incredible. He sent the disciples across the lake while He went to the mountainside to pray alone. Sometime later, something crazy happened. The winds started to get rough and the water picked up, rocking the boat back and forth. Then here comes Jesus walking on the water, always to the rescue.

> Now in the fourth watch of the night Jesus went to them, walking on the sea. And when the disciples saw Him walking on the sea, they were troubled, saying, "It is a ghost!" And they cried out for fear.
>
> But immediately Jesus spoke to them, saying, "Be of good cheer! It is I; do not be afraid."
>
> And Peter answered Him and said, "Lord, if it is You, command me to come to You on the water."
>
> So He said, "Come." And when Peter had come down out of the boat, he walked on the water to go to Jesus.
>
> Matthew 14:25–29 NKJV

Look again at how the disciples responded in their crisis. Terrified and crying out of fear, instead of seeing Jesus they saw a ghost. They could not recognize Him in the storm. What do you see when the storms of life hit you? Do you see Jesus, or do you see a ghost? When we allow doubt and unbelief to take over, we miss Jesus and see something else. We need to be like crazy Peter and step out of the boat and believe in the power of the Holy Spirit upon our lives in whatever circumstances we find ourselves today.

Let's make up our minds to drop-kick fear, doubt and unbelief. I thank God for Peter, that he saw the miracle for what it was and, because of it, was able to walk on water along with Jesus. If you are able to see Jesus in the storm, instead of drowning you will be walking on water with Him.

Selah. Stop and meditate.

Paul says this in Ephesians 6:10 (NKJV): "Finally, my brethren, be strong in the Lord and in the power of His might."

Satan is a master of whispers. We hear him whisper in our ears: "That is not Jesus in the storm; it is a ghost." As long as you let those whispers get into your ear, the deceiver will deceive you. I have one thing to say to you: Never doubt the power and authority of the living God. Believe what you see and see what you believe. It is not a ghost; it is Jesus, our risen Savior.

We live in times when it seems all hope is gone. So now we throw the word *hope* all over the place, hoping for something good to happen. We hear hope on social media; we hear hope on the news; we hear hope in the newspaper; we even hear hope from our politicians. We get fired up, encouraged about what we hear. We indeed may find ourselves holding on to temporary hope, but what is offered soon fades away, because what is offered in each of these messages is false hope. False hope gives us a moment of expectation for something good to happen, but in the end it fails.

The entire world is hungry for true hope. True hope is not just a feeling. Look again at the words of John 3:16 (KJV): "For God so loved the world, that he gave his only begotten Son, that whosoever believeth in him should not perish, but have everlasting life."

Has your human hope ever been crushed? Have you ever had an inner cry for real hope? Most of us have endured great sufferings and trials in our lives, and it causes us to lose our hope. Amazing books have been written about hope. We know of believers with powerful testimonies who have come through tragic hardships, and they encourage us and give us great faith—but even then our hope soon fades away.

Look at these powerful words from 1 Thessalonians 4:13–14 (NKJV): "I do not want you to be ignorant, brethren, concerning those who have fallen asleep, lest you sorrow as others who have no hope. For if we believe that Jesus died and rose again, even so God will bring with Him those who sleep in Jesus."

The book of Hebrews tells us that we have a hope set before us. I believe this hope is the Holy Spirit calling us to go deeper in relationship with Him. This hope that we have is an anchor of the soul—steadfast, immovable and unshakeable. I leave you with these words from Paul: "Now may the God of hope fill you with all joy and peace in believing, that you may abound in hope by the power of the Holy Spirit" (Romans 15:13 NKJV).

Hope is the work of the Holy Spirit, in us and through us. Not the hope of the world. The hope of the world is like a firecracker, here one moment and gone the next. There is a beautiful old hymn written by Edward Mote that goes like this: "My hope is built on nothing less / Than Jesus' blood and righteousness." These are the words that God promises us by faith in Christ's shed blood. The hope, peace and joy that come with it all lean on faith and our friendship with the Holy Spirit.

So why not take a time-out today. Take a deep breath, and invite the Holy Spirit into your heart—and make Him your best friend. You will never regret it.

10

The Mind of Christ

The book of Romans tells us:

> There is therefore now no condemnation to those who are in Christ Jesus, who do not walk according to the flesh, but according to the Spirit. For the law of the Spirit of life in Christ Jesus has made me free from the law of sin and death. . . . For to be carnally minded is death, but to be spiritually minded is life and peace. Because the carnal mind is enmity against God; for it is not subject to the law of God, nor indeed can be. So then, those who are in the flesh cannot please God.
>
> 8:1–2, 6–8 NKJV

Most believers are living their lives from the heart, the place of emotions. Where is the mind of Christ in the Body today? We are engrossed with our emotions, with whatever the heart says, but "the heart is deceitful above all things, and desperately wicked" (Jeremiah 17:9–10 NKJV).

We allow the devil to shut down our minds with anxiety, stress and worry. Fear overwhelms our thoughts, and we end up with an unsettled mind-set. We need to declare and decree this over our minds now:

> Be anxious for nothing, but in everything by prayer and supplication, with thanksgiving, let your requests be made known to God.
>
> Philippians 4:6 NKJV

Don't stop with that Scripture. Declare these words of Jesus over your mind, too:

> Come to Me, all you who labor and are heavy laden, and I will give you rest. Take My yoke upon you and learn from Me, for I am gentle and lowly in heart, and you will find rest for your souls.
>
> Matthew 11:28–29 NKJV

Punch the devil in the face and declare and decree this over yourself now:

> God has not given us a spirit of fear, but of power and of love and of a sound mind.
>
> 2 Timothy 1:7 NKJV

Kick the devil where it hurts and declare these two verses over your life now:

> [Cast] all your care upon [God], for He cares for you.
>
> 1 Peter 5:7 NKJV

> Have I not commanded you? Be strong and of good courage; do not be afraid, nor be dismayed, for the LORD your God is with you wherever you go.
>
> Joshua 1:9 NKJV

Get Off the Emotion Roller Coaster

We need to stop running to the emotions of our hearts. Listen to this metaphor of the roller-coaster ride: *The devil is the roller coaster, and the ride is your emotions.* You are depending on the highs and lows; you are being governed by your emotions and not the Holy Spirit. The devil will never attack your heart first, no way—he is going after your mind. The Bible says it is with the mind that we serve the Lord (I am just paraphrasing it). The Bible also says that we have the mind of Christ.

When the devil is fighting you in your mind, he is pushing the buttons of the emotions of your heart. You never win a battle with emotions; you simply expose yourself to the enemy. Never get into a spiritual-warfare fight with your feelings.

Where is the mind of Christ in the believer today? The devil wants to chop your head off spiritually. Your emotions will play out like a violin, and you will lose what God has for you. Victory is in your mind, not in your heart. You will lose the opportunities God has for your life if you give the devil free rein with your thoughts. And, believe me, he is trying to rob you of them. We have become very abstract in our thinking, just living from day to day in our emotions and feelings.

I will give you examples of how we sound. We say phrases like

- I don't know.
- I'm just not feeling it today.
- Well, maybe tomorrow.
- I might feel something later.
- I'm not in the mood today.
- I can't handle this anymore.
- I need to feel something.
- We will see what happens.

Every time you are on this roller coaster, you will lose God's opportunity for your life. We need to renew our minds with God's principles and promises.

Let the Holy Spirit govern your mind.

If you fail to allow this to take place in your life, you will be exempt from God's best. I can say this from the bottom of my heart. You can lose family, and it hurts; you can lose friends, and it hurts; you can lose money or a job, and it hurts. But never lose God's opportunities in your life because they are intertwined with your purpose and destiny. We can never forfeit them. Many of us lose the battle of the mind because we allow the heart to take over.

The devil has you so busy managing your feelings and emotions—things going on around and in you—that you are missing God and not growing spiritually. As I said before, many of us are like the church of Moses in the book of Numbers, which saw ten miracles of God's ultimate display of power in Egypt. God has done miracle after miracle in our lives, and we stall just like the Israelites in an emotional desert. For forty years they grew old, but they did not grow up spiritually. Many of us can relate, including myself. It is time to take off the garments of emotions and move into what God has for us, conquering our deliverance so we can receive our miracles.

Back in the Devil's Den—with Jesus

Let me share a story with you.

Some time ago my ministry was contacted by a Christian-based production company that wanted to do a documentary about my testimony. I agreed to it, and we went on this journey with the production team and headed to my old witchcraft places until we stopped at the ultimate demonic place in the Bronx, the witchcraft store—a place of pure hell.

I walked into the devil's den with the authority Jesus Christ had put on my life. I was fearless, untouchable and immovable, with a spiritual-warfare attitude. As the camera crew panned the merchandise, I exposed everything there, and how they were using these things to defeat the people who came into the store looking for help. From the statues the demons hide behind to all the other items there, they were satanic and demonic to the core. I went on a Holy Spirit rampage, and out of nowhere the camera guy panicked. He let his emotions grip him with fear.

He said to me, "Do you think it's safe to be here?"

At that very moment, I knew the devil had locked down his mind and was running with his emotions. He had to leave; he was that afraid. I was discouraged and disappointed. This was my only opportunity to go back to the devil's house and hit him where it hurts, exposing his true colors.

This was the place I went to as a devil worshiper to buy all my witchcraft tools, to perform witchcraft on people. Now, years later, I found myself on the other side of the cross, ready and able to do damage to the devil's camp, and I walked into the battlefield with someone who did not have the mind of Christ, who was not transformed to do battle, because it was all about how he felt that day.

I felt like the apostle Paul when he had the opportunity to go back and minister to the Sanhedrin. My mind was blown to go back to the place where I had bought satanic tools to fulfill the devil's plan. Now, here I was, back as a believer, to expose his dirty deeds.

Because this individual allowed the enemy to play on his heart like a grand piano in a symphony, the devil did so much damage to his life. He lost everything for a season—from his income to opportunities of blessing from the Lord. There was even friction brought into his marriage.

Let's get something straight. It was not because the devil was all-powerful; it was because the vessel was weak, and God allowed it to happen to teach my brother a lesson. Later, everything was restored back to him, praise be to God. I just wanted to share this story to let you know the consequences of our spiritual actions. This is not to put anyone down but to share the truth of the implications and consequences when we let the devil get the upper hand. Many of us are living heedlessly in our walks as Christians. It is time to separate our emotions and feelings from what we know from the Word of God.

Know one thing: The Holy Spirit is not the babysitter of your emotions, but the devil sure is. Cut the rope, renew your mind, wash your mind in the blood of Jesus Christ and be set free. It is time to conquer the deliverance of your mind. Kill the emotions of your natural man. The devil is not fighting you over your emotions but over your mind, giving you

- distorted images of who you are in Christ
- satanic imaginations
- threats of defeat and
- spiritual panic attacks to clog up your mind.

Time to get the Drano, which is the Holy Spirit, and unclog your mind. Stop letting your emotions run wild, because that is where the devil lives. My question to the Body of Christ is, Are you a Christian living without Jesus? Without the mind of Christ, that is what we are.

Without the mind of Christ, there will be

- no transformation of the mind
- no healing of the mind
- no spiritual understanding

- no walking in the Spirit
- no understanding of the Word of God and
- no taking Him at His Word.

My brother or sister, remember these words: "If anyone is in Christ, he is a new creation; old things have passed away; behold, all things have become new" (2 Corinthians 5:17 NKJV).

I share this one last thing with you. In order to conquer the deliverance of your mind and thoughts, understand this in your spirit: A conquering believer's mind-set is the state of being spiritually conscious and spiritually aware of the divine Word of God and of His presence in your life.

Meditate on God's Word. Live in it and let it be a lifestyle, and it will destroy your old desires as a carnal man. It will align you with the desires of God forever. Finally, it will bring awareness of God's opportunities for you that are intertwined with your purpose and destiny. God is a God of now. Don't miss this present moment He has for you as you walk with Him, in Jesus' name. Amen.

Take a moment to give God glory. This is the life that God has for you and me, to conquer our deliverance—in the unmatchable, untouchable name of Jesus Christ.

11

You Don't Bring a Knife to a Gunfight

As the old saying goes, "You don't bring a knife to a gunfight with the devil." You cannot bring yesterday's manna, yesterday's stories and yesterday's victories to the fight that is in front of you right now. It will not work.

Many believers get caught up with yesterday's fight and try to bring it to today's battle. That is the greatest mistake we can ever make. We try to fight the enemy with yesterday's anointing for today's battle. Yesterday's anointing was good for yesterday—and for yesterday's victory—but when we try to fight the new battles and new spiritual warfare of today, we learn a hard lesson: There are new levels and new devils.

With yesterday's memories, yesterday's testimonies or someone else's testimonies, we are hoping or thinking that we will get the victory today, but we are dead wrong, spiritually speaking.

In my witchcraft days, when I confronted Christians and went to battle against them, I always had the upper hand.

Not because their God was weak, but because they came to the fight with a spiritual knife when I had a spiritual gun. They came to the fight with old, ragged spiritual arsenals when I had the updated demonic artilleries to stop them in their tracks. They were frustrated and paralyzed spiritually. They could not go any further in the fight because they had no fresh anointing, no clarity in the spirit and no revelation in the heart about the fight. They also did not have a word from the Lord about how to engage the enemy because they took it upon themselves to engage in the spiritual-warfare battle on their own. They could not deal with or understand the satanic hindrance that came their way. They were not wise to the devil's devices.

The weapons that are used in the kingdom of darkness against every believer in Christ Jesus are weapons of

- hindrance
- delay
- blockage
- spiritual frustration and
- distraction.

These demonic arsenals will stop the spiritual progress of any believer who does not get a fresh word for the fight from the Lord Jesus Christ. For me to carry out these spiritual assaults, I had to create spiritual confusion around Christians, in places of their lives that led to no explanation. Under the powers of the dark side, I hit the Christian in his spiritual camp, where he prayed and fasted and trusted God. But he would have little or no results at all because he had no blueprint from the Lord on how to start the battle, finish the battle and win the battle.

The Significance of Storms

Have you ever noticed how many storms occur in the Bible? We know and understand from the Word that storms can be physical, spiritual, mental and emotional. Let me bring understanding about the storms.

> *Physical storms* are attacks against your body (sickness).
>
> *Spiritual storms* try to destroy your purpose and destiny.
>
> *Mental storms* are demonic attacks over your mind.
>
> *Emotional storms* are attacks against your spirit man and your relationship with the Holy Spirit.

We know from the book of Job, when the devil left the presence of God, he created a tornado, and the tornado killed Job's family. Great trials come to all who have truly given everything to Christ.

Psalm 34:19 (KJV) says, "Many are the afflictions of the righteous: but the LORD delivereth him out of them all."

No matter what happens, no matter what you are going through, let it be settled in your mind and in your heart that you will be sold out for Jesus Christ, whether you are on the mountaintop or in the valley. One of the things I would do when I confronted believers was use the past against them in the spiritual battle. I would use the past and their shortcomings, or their failures of yesterday—the guilt and shame that they had never surrendered to God.

It was an easy place in the mind to attack and to oppress and to create fear and havoc in believers' lives, using the memories of their past failures, their feelings of unworthiness and their consternation over why their prayers were not answered. Many brothers and sisters suffer because they do not know how to declutter their minds. My assignment was to punch and bring destructive hindrance into their lives. Now remove my face and you will see the devil at work in your (and my) life today.

Remember Paul's words: "Lest Satan should get an advantage of us: for we are not ignorant of his devices" (2 Corinthians 2:11 KJV).

The reality of this spiritual warfare is that we are going to be in the fight until the day we die, or when Jesus comes back to earth. We might be given seasons of rest, which are precious, but as long as we are on the earth, we need to engage the devil or he will engage us in this thing we call spiritual warfare. I thank God that we have been given the arsenals of heaven through the Holy Spirit.

> For though we walk in the flesh, we do not war after the flesh: (For the weapons of our warfare are not carnal, but mighty through God to the pulling down of strong holds;) casting down imaginations, and every high thing that exalteth itself against the knowledge of God, and bringing into captivity every thought to the obedience of Christ.
>
> 2 Corinthians 10:3–5 KJV

We have been equipped with weapons of heaven that the devil cannot withstand. Let me give a shout of hallelujah, because I believe it with all my heart! "Nor height, nor depth, nor any other creature, shall be able to separate us from the love of God, which is in Christ Jesus our Lord" (Romans 8:39 KJV).

So, devil, listen to me. Who shall separate me from the love of Christ Jesus? You think, devil, that tribulation, distress, persecution, famine or nakedness, peril or sword will? You must be crazy. Do you know that I am doing a life sentence in Jesus, and I want no parole? Do you know that I am on death row with Christ? So there is neither principality, nor demon, nor hell, nor demonic spirit, nor witch, nor warlock that can separate me from my purpose and destiny in Christ Jesus and the love of God!

Your Holy Ghost Machine Gun for the Fight

The message to you in your spiritual battle is clear. Hear these words of Scripture: "But ye, beloved, building up yourselves on your most holy faith, praying in the Holy Ghost, keep yourselves in the love of God, looking for the mercy of our Lord Jesus Christ unto eternal life" (Jude 20–21 KJV).

It is time to bring it to the devil once and for all. Know one thing—and you can hang your hat on this: God is all-powerful and His Word declares truth and brings results. You pray these prayers and every demonic mountain of hindrance, delay, blockage, spiritual frustration and distraction will be destroyed by the fire of the Holy Spirit.

Let's not be like the sons of Sceva.

> Then some of the itinerant Jewish exorcists took it upon themselves to call the name of the Lord Jesus over those who had evil spirits, saying, "We exorcise you by the Jesus whom Paul preaches." Also there were seven sons of Sceva, a Jewish chief priest, who did so.
>
> And the evil spirit answered and said, "Jesus I know, and Paul I know; but who are you?"
>
> Then the man in whom the evil spirit was leaped on them, overpowered them, and prevailed against them, so that they fled out of that house naked and wounded.
>
> Acts 19:13–16 NKJV

Learn from the sons of Sceva. When you come to the fight, bring the right weapons, not anyone else's weapons. As I said before, Jesus Christ is all-powerful. It is time to put the devil on notice and break everything that is trying to bring destruction into your life. Get ready to pick up your spiritual machine gun and have no mercy—fire away.

Prayer Arsenals

Father, thank You for Your mighty right hand that is working in my behalf in Jesus' name.

I praise and worship Your holy name.

I know that no matter what the devil says, You always hear my prayers spoken in Jesus' name.

Let every demonic mountain that is in front of me be destroyed, in Jesus' name.

I release the fire of the Holy Spirit against every road-block in my life, in Jesus' name.

I command the fire of the Holy Spirit to strike down every hindrance, delay and distraction in my life.

Every mountain of shame be cast into the sea, in Jesus' name.

Every mountain of sickness be removed now, in Jesus' name.

I destroy, by the fire of the Holy Spirit, every delay in my life, in Jesus' name.

I confuse and change the languages of every demonic network that is operating to steal my purpose and destiny, in Jesus' name.

I break and destroy every demonic alignment that is trying to come into my life, in Jesus' name.

Let the fire of God break and destroy every demonic meeting against me, in Jesus' name.

I bind and rebuke all demonic reinforcements against me, in Jesus' name.

I rebuke every hindrance and spiritual frustration in my life, in the name of Jesus.

Every hindering spirit, receive the judgments of God upon your head, in Jesus' name.

Every spirit of blockage that is stopping me from reaching my promised land, let the judgments of God fall upon your head.

Every spirit that is trying to kill my destiny, the fire of God be released now to destroy you all.

Let every astral-projecting devil fall to the ground, in Jesus' name.

Every satanic entrapment, die now, in the name of Jesus.

Begin to praise God and give Him the glory. Worship Him for your supernatural breakthrough.

12

Which Fight Is Mine?

Have you ever had a spiritual battle that starts small and then increases as the days, weeks and months go by? There is an important principle about spiritual warfare that we can glean from the life of David, Israel's greatest king. David's life is an awesome example of discerning which fight was his. David had certain strategic tactics down to a science before he headed into battle—whether he was fighting off a lion or a Philistine. He made it his business to ask God, "Is this my battle?" or "Is this my fight? Should I pursue my enemy?"

David grew up learning the best strategies and maneuvered to win the fight. As we mentioned earlier, he grew up as the youngest son in his father's house, taking care of the flock of sheep and keeping them safe from wild animals. The most effective weapon David used—and we should take a page from his spiritual-warfare book—was *listening to the voice of God*.

Listening to the voice of the Lord here and there, however, is not enough. We must stay tuned in to God's voice because the enemy has a trick up his sleeves. He will send a counterfeit attack to see if you take the bait. It is like in a football game:

The opponents try to get the opposite team to jump over the line prematurely, and then it gets penalized. Instead of gaining ground, they lose ground. Many of us today experience this in the spirit realm. Then, when the real fight shows up, we are too spiritually exhausted to take care of business. Now it takes twice the time to gain the ground back from the enemy as we move deeper into the battle.

Always know one thing: Every spiritual-warfare fight is like Double Dutch jump rope—you have to know when to jump in and when to jump out. This only happens by hearing God's voice, knowing His voice and staying connected to His voice so you have no spiritual setbacks in the fight. In a spiritual-warfare assault, the enemy is very good at convincing us to bring into the battlefield the same strategies we used in the last fight. We have made a bad judgment because we won the battle yesterday, last week or last year with the arsenals God provided for victory in that season and time. So we think we have the Lord Jesus Christ figured out, and we bring yesterday's victory, yesterday's manna (a dried-up word, not a fresh one), yesterday's fasting— and we do not bring a fresh anointing into a fight that is of a different realm of the spirit.

Don't Put God in a Box

There is a Christian saying we have used so many times it has become a cliché: "New levels, new devils." If I could get a nickel for every time I have heard these words, I would be a rich man. We quote that to ourselves, or we quote it to others, so why is it that we bring yesterday's strategies or yesterday's arsenals or yesterday's spiritual warfare to a new level of the battle? In other words, don't put God in a box.

Let me prove something to you. David went to take lunch to his brothers and got himself into a fight. The Bible says that

David was armed and dangerous with a slingshot; we know that he went into the battlefield that day with just five stones to use against the giant called Goliath. As David prepared for the fight, King Saul tried to give him his armor, and David went so far as to put it on. But David knew in his spirit that this was not the armor and weapon for that moment in that time. So what did he do? David took off what was not his.

In the same way today, you may be tempted to put on someone else's praise report or someone else's testimony, but that is not for you or your fight with the giant that is in your land. David took what was his—the slingshot and five stones that God gave him—and ran down to the battlefield and made history.

What stones has God given you for your fight?

David understood in his spirit how to fight the good fight of faith. And we know how the story goes: David had many battles and wars in his life, but he never went back to using the slingshot again. We need to learn from King David. What is your fight, and what is your battle, and what is God saying to you? A crucial mistake we make is to run for spiritual advice; we run to our pastors and intercessors to find a game plan, but we leave the Lord Jesus Christ out of the equation for the instructions we need from heaven. One thing I know from my walk with the Lord is that every spiritual-warfare fight has a purpose in the spirit realm and in our lives. The only way to define the purpose for which you are entering into the battle is this:

Do not enter into the fight (spiritual-warfare battle) unless God has given you the blueprint or steps to conquer your enemies.

The battle brings many spiritual elements; it could be recovering your health, your finances, your marriage, your ministry, your church, your family, your career. Whatever the purpose, as you engage in spiritual warfare you must identify the area that

God wants you to conquer. It is not about praying a thousand different ways; you need precision-targeted prayers to bring down targets in the enemy's camp in order to take back what he has stolen from you.

Let me share some crucial instructions before you confront the enemy, or your Goliath. Many believers today, including myself, have lost some spiritual battles, not because God was weak or not in it, but because we missed hearing the spiritual-warfare instructions from the Holy Spirit. So instead of being victorious, we became casualties of war.

In my walk with the Lord Jesus Christ, before I engage in the fight—before I take it to the enemy—I have learned to do a spiritual assessment that I call dressing up for the battle, which ensures that my spiritual armor is on tight. In other words, how is my relationship with the Holy Spirit? Do I have any sins lingering around me, causing me to go into the battle half-dressed? I check my lifestyle and my walk with Jesus. I make sure that my heart is right, that I do not carry anything that displeases God, and that I am living a sincere and genuine life with Him.

Dressing Up for Battle: Seven Spiritual Principles

Let me give you seven spiritual principles that I pray will give you clarity and revelation in your heart.

Purpose

Spiritual warfare must have a purpose. What is yours? You will find that out only by the Holy Spirit speaking to you.

Instructions

Get your marching orders, or spiritual instructions, before you engage in spiritual warfare. Make sure this is your fight and that you are in tune with the voice of the Holy Spirit. Make sure you know the spiritual season you are in and the one you are going into.

Spiritual Checkup

Is your walk part-time, or is it a lifestyle? Put another way, are you a Christian Dior—a wannabe believer—or a true believer in Jesus Christ?

Is there any unrepented area of sin in your life?

Are you totally surrendered to the Lord Jesus Christ?

Preparation

A life in Christ is a life of fasting and prayer. Jesus said in the Word that some devils come out only by fasting and praying. Let me share with you that some spiritual battles can only be won by fasting and prayer, too. A combination of these two disciplines creates a one-two punch in the devil's face.

Faith

How is your faith? Is your faith in the ICU? Is your faith crippled? Jesus said that if you have faith the size of a mustard seed, you can tell that mountain to be cast into the sea. Let me share a quick insight with you. If your faith is crippled, you will not be victorious in the fight. But if your faith is the size of a mustard seed and is stubborn faith, the devil is in trouble. Be spiritually relentless and tenacious and be consistent on the battlefield.

Aggressiveness

Make sure you are aggressive on the battlefield and have determination against the enemy of your soul. It is time to overpower him and be aggressive against the kingdom of darkness.

Holiness

A life of holiness is living in obedience to Jesus Christ and His Word. If you live a consecrated (holy) life, you will always have the spiritual strength you need to fight the good fight of faith against the wiles and schemes of the devil.

These are the key points to living a victorious life against the devil and his kingdom.

When Warfare Gets Real

One day many years ago, I was ministering at a conference in Florida. I was still a young believer and just starting out in part-time ministry. Toward the end of the conference, I happened to notice a particular young lady sitting in the crowd. As the conference ended, I went to the back of the church to pack up my books—at the time I had only one book, *Out of the Devil's Cauldron*, which is my testimony. Suddenly I heard screams coming from the main room where the conference had just ended. It was a crazy commotion with people yelling, "Come out in the name of Jesus!" It got louder and louder as I kept packing my bag; this went on for quite a while.

Sometime later I heard my name being called out: "Call John!" At that moment it hit me in my spirit that something serious was going on with the devil. I confess I was so spiritually exhausted I was ignoring it. I did not want to be involved because I knew this situation was crazier than a fruitcake.

As I went into the main conference room, I saw the young lady stretched out and levitating off the floor, as she was demon-possessed. Pastors and bishops were all around her, trying to hold her down. She had the supernatural strength of one hundred men, and she was only five-foot-one and about 120 pounds. Screams such as I never heard before were coming out of her, with the demon shouting, "I'm going to kill her tonight!"

As these pastors and bishops were trying to hold her down with all their strength, and trying to cast the devil out of her, the demon said, "You can call anyone you want. I am not going to come out. I don't care what name you call." I was shocked and dumbfounded that these men and women of God were calling on Jesus to cast out this demon, and the demon just laughed and mocked them.

As I touched the young lady, I heard the Holy Spirit say to me, *Tell them to let her go.* When I told them this, they thought I was out of my mind because she had demonic strength. One thing I knew about myself (not judging them) was that I lived a life of holiness, and I had crazy, stubborn faith. I was spiritually aggressive and prepared for the battle, and I had my instructions straight from the Holy Spirit.

The demons let her go. As I knelt down in front of the demonically possessed girl, all I saw were the whites of her eyes, as her pupils were rolled back in her head. I put my hand on her forehead, and her eyes rolled back down like a slot machine in a Las Vegas casino, and the pupils returned to normal.

The words that came out of this demon-possessed young lady—she had the voice of a man—were, "You I know."

All I said to that devil was, "You don't know me because I am a new creation in Christ Jesus. But you come out now, in the name of Jesus."

Horrific sounds came out of her mouth, and the demon was gone. Praise be to God that she was set free.

This is how you win the battle by the power of the Holy Spirit and the spiritual principles I shared with you above. Know one thing, and I leave you with this: Discern which fight is yours, and you will have the last laugh in Jesus Christ against the enemy called the devil.

13

The Devil Does Not Play

The devil is not your friend. Did you hear me? Wake up! It is not a matter of *if* he is going to strike you; it is a matter of *when*.

I heard a story once about a scorpion that was trying to get to the other side of a lake. He stopped and had a conversation with a frog. He said, "Hello, Mr. Frog, how are you today?" He engaged the frog in a conversation—big mistake for the frog. It is the same way when the devil engages believers in a conversation—big mistake.

But I will continue with my story. The scorpion told the frog, "What a lovely day today." There were blue skies and sunshine. The scorpion said, "What d'you say, Mr. Frog?" The number-one entrapment of the enemy is to engage you in a conversation.

The frog said, "Yes, Mr. Scorpion, we have beautiful skies and a sunshiny day." This is how the devil draws you in, because he is trying to get something from you.

The scorpion said, "By the way, Mr. Frog, do you find yourself to be busy today?" This is the enemy setting up the entrapment.

Sensing the need for caution, and a little bit intimidated, the frog replied, "Not really, why do you ask?"

The scorpion said, "I seem to have a dilemma, and I was hoping you could help me on this beautiful day."

This is what the devil does to many believers today—he paints a pretty picture.

The frog hesitated but finally said, "What is your dilemma, Mr. Scorpion?"

The scorpion replied, "It's just a simple thing that I request." This is just like the devil, setting up the believer to make him think that what is happening at the moment is something small. Then later on you have no way out.

The scorpion then said, "I would like to get to the other side of the lake and visit some friends. Do you think, Mr. Frog, that you can help me?" He said this with a demonic grin on his face, looking polite and humble at the same time. This is what the devil does to the Church at large—presenting something that seems so innocent but is deadly spiritually.

The frog was too intimidated to respond to the scorpion's request. Many of us are intimidated to confront the enemy head on. The frog took a second or two and finally said, "Mr. Scorpion, if I agree to help you and bring you to the other side of the lake, I know you are going to sting me, and I will die."

The scorpion hesitated a beat, looked the frog straight in the eyes and said, "Why would I do that to you when you are willing to help me out to visit my precious friends? I promise you and give you my word that I will not do such a thing to you."

Know one thing, the devil does not negotiate, and he plays for keeps.

The Snare of the Fowler

Psalm 91 describes the fowler, which is the devil, and the four entrapments of the enemy. The deadliest of the entrapments is the young lion. This is a metaphor of the sin we think we can play with and put away anytime we want to. This is the devil's game, and he does not negotiate.

James 1:15–16 (NIV) explains: "Then, after desire has conceived, it gives birth to sin; and sin, when it is full-grown, gives birth to death. Don't be deceived, my dear brothers and sisters."

The frog decided to let the scorpion sit on his back and take him safely across the lake. As they swam across the lake, the frog was cautious and fearful at the same time. As they approached the halfway point of the journey, the scorpion stung the frog.

Shocked, the frog turned to the scorpion and said, "Why would you do a thing like that when you promised me you wouldn't sting me?"

The scorpion smiled and said, "It is in my nature to lie. I can't help myself, and that's why I did what I did."

This is who the enemy is; this is his true identity. He is deceptive and cunning, and the Bible makes it clear in John 10:10 that the devil has one mission—to steal, kill and destroy—but his tactics are limited. Jesus came to give us life and give life in abundance. Even though the devil's tactics are limited, he will use them in clever and deceitful ways to try to accomplish his mission to keep us from the abundant life that Jesus Christ has bought for us by the finished work of the cross. We do not want to be like Mr. Frog. Sadly, the Church today has become just like Mr. Frog in associating and compromising with the enemy of our souls.

As I mentioned earlier, my friend Pastor Bill from First Love Ministries describes the Church as a type of Samson, lying in the lap of Delilah, a type of the world. I will go a step further and say that Delilah is a type of the devil, and we are playing the violin and singing the devil's songs when God has called us to be the true worshipers.

117

There was a story in the witchcraft world, where I lived for 25 years, of a man and the violin. This man was so desperate to play the violin that he was willing to pay the ultimate price, no matter what it cost him. It is like the believer who wants something so badly and wants to be blessed at any cost that it does not matter who shows up and blesses him. The biggest mistake that the devil wants you to make is to take your eyes off Jesus' face and place them on his hands instead. This is called the "gimme" mentality. I am entitled to it.

The man who wanted to play the violin heard a voice one day that said, "Meet me in the forest, and I will make you a master player of the violin." He kissed his family that morning and said, "I will be back in a couple of hours," and off he went on his journey to meet this mystery man (the devil does not negotiate).

Once he was in the forest, the man was taught how to play the violin in a matter of seconds, minutes and hours. An incredible sound came out of the forest, and he ran home to share the news with his family. As he approached the door of his home, there was a man on the other side of the open doorway, and to his shock the stranger said, "Can I help you, sir?"

The man with the violin responded, "This is my home."

The stranger said, "No, I don't think so."

The man said, "Call Sally, my wife, and she will testify that I live here and that she is my wife." When Sally came to the door, she was shocked to see the man standing there.

The man said, "Honey, do you remember me?"

She answered, "I thought something happened to you because you never came back."

He replied, "Baby, I was only gone for one day."

She looked him straight in the eyes and said, "No, you are wrong. You have been gone for twenty years." So the man lost everything. He lost his home, his wife and his family because of what he wanted so badly.

Many Christians today lose their purpose and destiny and above all their relationship with the Lord Jesus Christ. Even the Church at large has gone into the forest and lost its mission on the earth. But that should not be the end of our story. It is time to get back to the perfect will of God.

> Finally, be strong in the Lord and in his mighty power. Put on the full armor of God, so that you can take your stand against the devil's schemes. For our struggle is not against flesh and blood, but against the rulers, against the authorities, against the powers of this dark world and against the spiritual forces of evil in the heavenly realms. Therefore, put on the full armor of God, so that when the day of evil comes, you may be able to stand your ground, and after you have done everything, to stand.
>
> Ephesians 6:10–13 NIV

The Ministry of Violence

Let me introduce you to what I call the ministry of violence. If you think that sounds strange, know that I get it straight from Scripture. Do you remember this puzzling verse? "And from the days of John the Baptist until now the kingdom of heaven suffers violence, and the violent take it by force" (Matthew 11:12 NKJV).

Listen to me, my brother and sister, and listen carefully. When Lucifer was in heaven and evil was found in his heart, he campaigned and petitioned for the support of many angels to overthrow God. But God always has a plan. I tell you from the place of a broken heart that the devil is campaigning for your support. Let me introduce you to the ministry of fire, violence and terror that will destroy the enemy's camp.

Today there should be a ministry in all churches, front and center, that will destroy the works of the devil. Exodus 15:3

119

(NKJV) says, "The LORD is a man of war; the LORD is His name." Why then are we playing patty-cake with the devil? It is time to get violent and ugly against the devil and his kingdom—his schemes, wiles and demonic plots.

Writing to his beloved spiritual son, Timothy, the apostle Paul said:

> I have fought the good fight, I have finished the race, I have kept the faith. Finally, there is laid up for me the crown of righteousness, which the Lord, the righteous Judge, will give to me on that Day, and not to me only but also to all who have loved His appearing.
>
> 2 Timothy 4:7–8 NKJV

If you want this to be your life, purpose and destiny and how you want to finish your race, too, stop playing games with the devil. It is time to get ugly on the devil. Declare these two Scriptures before we get into the spiritual-warfare fight.

> Here am I and the children whom the LORD has given me! We are for signs and wonders in Israel from the LORD of hosts, who dwells in Mount Zion.
>
> Isaiah 8:18 NKJV

> Most assuredly, I say to you, he who believes in Me, the works that I do he will do also; and greater works than these he will do, because I go to My Father.
>
> John 14:12 NKJV

Prayer Points

Are you ready? Let's pray in faith together. The devil will hate you for this. So what.

120

Jesus, You are all-powerful, and I thank You for the anointing upon my life.

Father God, You anointed Your Son, Jesus Christ, with the Holy Spirit and power. Do the same for me before I go into battle, in Jesus' name.

Father, as You were with Jesus, be with me today, in Jesus' name. Thank You.

Lord, let the power of the Holy Spirit rest upon me in a new way, in Jesus' name.

Holy Spirit, fill me with a fresh anointing now, in Jesus' name.

Holy Spirit, let Your hand lead my hand into battle, in Jesus' name.

Let every demonic attack that is looking to destroy or contaminate my anointing die by the fire of the Holy Spirit, in Jesus' name.

Lord, make me a vessel of deliverance in Your hands, in Jesus' name.

Lord, use me today the same way You used Elijah. Let the fire of God terrify the enemy's camp, in Jesus' name.

Holy Spirit, as You worked through Jesus Christ, work through me today.

Let the fire of the Holy Spirit reign upon and through me to destroy the works of the enemy, in Jesus' name.

I dip myself in the blood of Jesus Christ and the anointing of the Holy Spirit, in Jesus' name.

Father God, let every demon tremble, in Jesus' name.

Holy Spirit, do signs, wonders and miracles in and through my life, in Jesus' name.

Father God, may your deliverance and healing power flow through me, in Jesus' name, today and forever.

I destroy every compromise, negotiation and demonic contract known and unknown, in Jesus' name.

Let every wicked spirit of the mountains, valleys, forests, seas and oceans that is trying to rob my anointing be destroyed, in Jesus' name.

Let every demon that I compromised with be destroyed, in Jesus' name.

Let every demonic spirit that I made peace, contracts and alliances with be destroyed by the fire of the Holy Spirit.

I destroy every demonic allegiance, pact, contract, covenant and agreement that I made with the dark side—the devil, witches and warlocks, and the occult; let them be destroyed today in the name of Jesus.

Holy Spirit, I am nothing without You, in Jesus' name.

Lord Jesus, manifest Your power and glory so the kingdom of darkness may know that You are God, and I am Your servant, in Jesus' name.

Thank You, Holy Spirit, for working through me. I love You forever, in Jesus' name.

Give God glory and praise for your victory today. Amen.

14

Conquering Your Dreams

We need to understand the blueprint of the enemy's kingdom—his tactics, entrapments and strongholds, and ultimately the bondage he tries to incarcerate believers with. You cannot defeat him when you do not understand what you are dealing with. We need insight into the devil's game plan upon your life and mine. I get so much email throughout the year describing how precious brothers and sisters are under attack throughout the night.

Back when I served the dark side, we would call it the "night season." Many of us today have experienced demonic dreams in every facet and form. Many of us could testify that we sleep, but we do not get rest. We are warring throughout the night in our dreams. It is time to destroy all satanic dreams.

Listen to these words from Scripture: "While everyone was sleeping, his enemy came and sowed weeds among the wheat, and went away. When the wheat sprouted and formed heads, then the weeds also appeared" (Matthew 13:25–26 NIV).

In this very hour, Satan has unleashed thousands of evil spirits of the highest rank to sow destruction and plant demonic seeds and entrapments through your dreams. The enemy's number-one agenda in the realm of your dreams is to monitor your spiritual life and bring destruction and darkness and enslave you.

Many believers fail to be prayed up and to release their worries and cares to the Lord before they go to bed. If you learn to conquer your dreams, however, you will receive the peace of God before you lay your head on the pillow at night.

Unmask the Enemy

These demons masquerade themselves in numerous ways. They chase you in dreams as spirit husbands or wives to have sexual encounters with you so they can seduce you and have sex with you in your dreams. You might have dreams where you have been shot and killed, or demonic dreams of rape that are so real you wake up screaming at that very moment. These demonic dreams are portals into the unseen world. Many times what happens in your dreams is staged to affect, to influence satanically, your life outside in the natural realm. The devil infiltrates dreams to bring destructions of every kind. You might have incubus and succubus demons, demonic soul ties in your dreams, demonic weddings in your dreams, dreams that you are in an operating room—a demonic surgery—and even dreams of premature death.

An incubus is a demon in male form that lies with women in order to have sexual intercourse with them. Its counterpart is the succubus, which is a female demon believed to have sexual intercourse with men while they are sleeping. You may see yourself spiritually pregnant as you have these demonic encounters in your dreams. These demons bring destruction of abortion, miscarriage, barrenness and even death.

The sexual dreams bring perversion, witchcraft and manipulation. There are also other demonic dreams of witchcraft spells, demonic altars with your name and picture on them, and demonic ceremonies and rituals. You may see yourself bathing in animal/human blood, or you may see yourself dressed up in white surrounded by people you do not even know. There are also demonic dreams of people chasing you who are trying to kill you, and you do not even know why.

These are setups and entrapments of the enemy to set you up in the natural realm for premature death. The devil uses these entrapments and attacks in the night season, when you lay your head on the pillow.

In the demonic world where I lived for 25 years, it was called "catching you off guard." Many Christians do not understand the spiritual warfare that happens in their dreams, and it usually happens when they least expect it. The sad thing about it is that for a believer, it can be a spiritual deathblow, because when we get up that morning, instead of renouncing and cursing it to the root, we carry this curse of a dream throughout the day by speaking into it and giving it authority and attention, giving it demonic power and giving the devil our undivided attention. You run to every intercessor and every so-called prophet to interpret the dream, to your demise. The devil is setting you up by increasing his demonic arsenals against you to bring you down to nothing in the natural.

Arsenal Prayer Points

It is time to wake up spiritually through these powerful prayers.

Breaking the Devil's Arsenals

Father God, I thank You for the blood of Jesus that cleanses and protects me from all evil.

Lord, I thank You for preparing a table before me in the presence of my enemies, the demons who operate in the night season.

I thank You that You give rest to those who fear Your name.

As I lie down and fall asleep, I shall have rest from the Lord, and I fear no demonic attacks in my dreams.

Let those that are chasing and attacking me in my dreams and in my life be cut off, in the name of Jesus.

Let every spiritual gun, bullet, arrow and fire against me break and be destroyed, in the name of Jesus.

Let every spiritual assassin that is trying to hunt me down in my dreams be destroyed, in the name of Jesus.

Let every satanic firing squad that has tried to take me out die, in the name of Jesus.

I stand behind the blood of Jesus and the finished work of the cross against every demonic bullet fired at me, in the powerful name of Jesus.

Every witchcraft weapon that has been assigned against me, let it shrivel up and die, in the name of Jesus.

Time to Fight Back

I pick up the arsenals of heaven, and I thank God for exposing the tactics of the enemy that God has revealed to me through my dreams.

Now, place your hand on your head and cancel every demonic dream you ever had, in the name of Jesus.

I reject every satanic dream, in the name of Jesus.

Lord, take me into Your presence right now, and by the fire of the Holy Spirit, destroy every satanic dream in the spirit world against me, in Jesus' name.

I arrest every spiritual attacker and paralyze every satanic attack in my dreams, in the name of Jesus.

Every satanic seed that has been planted in my dreams, be uprooted and pulled out now, in the name of Jesus.

Let all satanic manipulations through every dream I ever had be destroyed, in the name of Jesus.

Holy Spirit, let Your fire purge me and make me whole, inside and out, now, in the name of Jesus.

I break every evil covenant through any demonic dream, in the name of Jesus.

I release the fire of the Holy Spirit to quench every fiery dart now, in the name of Jesus.

Let every evil plan in my "night season" dreams be destroyed by the fire of God before daybreak, in the name of Jesus.

Arsenals of Heaven Destroying Sexual Demons

Let the fire of God fall upon every sexual demon in my dreams, in the name of Jesus.

Incubus demon, may the fire of God destroy you right now, in the name of Jesus.

Succubus demon, may the fire and thunder of God destroy you right now, in the name of Jesus.

I command all sexual demons by the authority of Jesus to come out, now, in the name of Jesus.

I cut down by the sword of the Holy Spirit every sexual demon out of my life, now, in the name of Jesus.

Incubus, I castrate you by the fire of God, now, in Jesus' name.

Succubus, I command the judgments of God to come down on your private parts, now, in the name of Jesus.

I reject all sexual advances from incubus and succubus in my dreams. Let them burn up and die, in Jesus' name.

I destroy all demons of seduction and sexual advances against me, in the name of Jesus.
I refuse to give my body to any demon in my dreams. My body is the temple of the Holy Spirit, in Jesus' name.

Say this Scripture out loud:

For the idols have spoken vanity, and the diviners have seen a lie, and have told false dreams; they comfort in vain: therefore they went their way as a flock, they were troubled, because there was no shepherd.

Zechariah 10:2 KJV

Prayer Points of Destruction

Let's destroy the enemy once and for all with these prayer points:

God, I believe that You are the only one who can give true dreams today.
I will receive only the dreams that come from God and my Lord Jesus Christ.
Holy Spirit, put me in stealth mode, and do not allow the devil and his demons to know my location in my dreams, in Jesus' name.
Let every filthy dream be destroyed, in the name of Jesus.
Let every filthy dreamer in my dreams be destroyed, in the name of Jesus.
Lord, lay Your right hand upon my head as I go to sleep, in Jesus' name.
My dreams are directed by God to guide my life into my purpose and destiny, in Jesus' name.
Tonight, I declare and decree that I will dream good dreams, in Jesus' name.
Let every demonic barrier be destroyed, in Jesus' name.

Let every evil altar and cauldron set against me in my dream be destroyed by the blood of Jesus.

Let every demon that is trying to suck my blood and do satanic rituals in my dreams be cursed to the root, in the name of Jesus.

I call upon the fire of the Holy Spirit to destroy every evil image in my dreams, in Jesus' name.

Let every evil power that the devil is trying to use against me be destroyed now, in the name of Jesus.

I refuse to submit to any evil powers, in the name of Jesus.

I refuse to fly in my dreams tonight, in the name of Jesus.

Let every satanic attack against me in my dreams be burned up by the fire of the Holy Spirit.

Let every demonic spirit of seduction, lust, fornication, adultery, prostitute spirits, Jezebel and Delilah spirits be brought down and destroyed by the fire of God, in Jesus' name.

Let every spiritual wife and husband in my dreams be caged by the Holy Spirit, in Jesus' name.

I reject all demonic marriage certificates; let them burn up now, in the name of Jesus.

I reject all demonic wedding rings that were given to me in my dreams; let them be destroyed, in Jesus' name.

I will not partake of or attend any spiritual weddings in my dreams, in the name of Jesus.

Take a few minutes right now to praise God for your deliverance, for your peace and for your joy over your dreams tonight and forevermore, in the name of Jesus.

Declare and decree this psalm over your life now:

The Lord is my light and my salvation—whom shall I fear? The Lord is the stronghold of my life—of whom shall I be afraid?

When the wicked advance against me to devour me, it is my enemies and my foes who will stumble and fall. Though an army besiege me, my heart will not fear; though war break out against me, even then I will be confident.

One thing I ask from the LORD, this only do I seek: that I may dwell in the house of the LORD all the days of my life, to gaze on the beauty of the LORD and to seek him in his temple. For in the day of trouble he will keep me safe in his dwelling; he will hide me in the shelter of his sacred tent and set me high upon a rock.

Psalm 27:1–5 NIV

Astral-Projecting Demons

Let us not forget to deal with the astral-projecting demons and destroy their demonic arsenals once and for all, in the name of Jesus. When I was in the demonic world, I had contracts and covenants where demons would give me the ability to astral project.

What is astral projecting? Many people ask that today. Simply put, astral projecting is an out-of-body experience of high-level occult members where they perform with demonic powers. It has to do with traveling spiritually in different regions, countries and neighborhoods. These devils can even astral project into your home for the purpose to do you harm.

When a person astral projects, the person's spirit is separated from his or her material body through satanic powers during out-of-body travels. The demon empowers the person, as there is a powerful connection between the person and the demon; they are connected in the physical and spiritual realms at the same time. This is what they call the silver cord. In spiritual warfare, if you destroy the silver cord—which is the contract between the demon and the person—there is a great possibility the person will not return back to his body, which will result in physical death. The demonic mission will then be completely destroyed.

Let's aim our arsenals into the spirit realm to destroy every astral-projecting devil, in the name of Jesus. Let's stop them in their tracks. Open your mouth and repeat after me:

Heavenly Father, hear my voice! I declare and decree and put the judgments of God upon every evil spirit working against me, in the name of Jesus.

Holy Spirit, send Your fire of judgment upon every astral-projecting devil that is trying to bring destruction into my life, in Jesus' name.

Holy Spirit, let every agent of darkness that is astral projecting against me be brought down, in the name of Jesus.

Let the cross of Jesus Christ stand in the way of every agent of darkness astral projecting into my dreams or into my home. Let them be brought down, in the name of Jesus.

I destroy every satanic timing and traveling ability that is looking to destroy me, in the name of Jesus.

Every person astral projecting to carry out evil against my home, my family, my finances, my career and destiny, I cut their silver cord now, in the name of Jesus.

Let the angels of God intercept every traveling witch and warlock that is trying to come against my neighborhood, home and region. Let the fire of God burn them down to the ground, in Jesus' name.

I come against every evil mandate now, in the name of Jesus.

Every demonic power traveling to monitor my life, I send the fire of God to burn it down from the sky, in Jesus' name.

Every witch astral projecting into my house, my apartment, my bedroom, I paralyze you with the blood of Jesus.

Every warlock that is astral projecting into my church and ministry, let the assignment be brought down, in the name of Jesus.

Let the silver cord be cut off—and every satanic agent that has been assigned to destroy my life, let that mission be destroyed now, in Jesus' name.

Father, I send Your judgments against every astral-projecting devil that is trying to destroy me after the midnight hour, in the name of Jesus.

Let the fire of the Holy Spirit be sent and take vengeance against all my enemies that are astral projecting against me tonight, in the name of Jesus.

Take a moment to praise God for the victory over your life in Jesus' name.

Good Dreams Are from God

I want to share my testimony of how I conquered my dreams. Many of my precious brothers and sisters in the Christian family, here and around the world, know my story—that I came from hell to church—and the journey has not been easy. From the church letting me down to brothers—who at one time treated me like kin—plotting to betray me on a Ponzi scheme, where I lost everything, it has been a bumpy ride.

I told you in chapter 3 how, for two nights in a row, sitting on a rock in Flushing Meadow Park in Queens, I heard one of the greatest evangelists of all times, Billy Graham, preach the Gospel as I ate a ham-and-cheese sandwich with the summer breeze on my face. I heard two of the greatest messages I have ever heard preached. And later I had the privilege and honor to know Pastor David Wilkerson, whom God placed in my life to mentor me for three years. A short time later, I met one of the most incredible evangelists of our time, the Reverend Nicky Cruz.

When I was a young believer in my first church, people would come up to me and say, "You will be an evangelist, John. God has called you to be an evangelist." I heard that so many times, but I had no idea or clue what it really meant. I guess somehow they knew something that I did not know at the time. I know that God gives prophetic dreams; it is all over the Bible, especially in the Old Testament. God spoke to the saints of old through visions and dreams.

Allow me to stop for a minute and share something out of the box. I have had many demonic dreams over the past two decades in which devil worshipers try their hardest to get me back into the satanic world by infiltrating my dreams and trying to seduce me through spiritual cleansings and ceremonies. In every dream, without a miss, I held my ground and preached the Gospel in their demonic rituals and ceremonies. Not even once were they able to lay their demonic hands on me. I got the victory, and I conquered my dreams.

Fast-forward throughout my young Christian walk, when the words that I would be an evangelist kept popping up everywhere I went. All I ever wanted to do was serve God and finish my race. I never thought I would be involved in anything that had to do with ministry. To be honest, it was getting a little boring and tiring to hear people repeat themselves so many times. Then one day I sought the Lord and asked about all these people telling me that someday I would be an evangelist.

I told the Lord, "I want to know what You have to say, since You are the One who called and saved me, not the people. So I want to know, what is an evangelist, and is this my calling?"

Sometime later, one night, I had this amazing dream:

In the dream I ended up in Nicky Cruz's home, and we were going back and forth and having this amazing conversation. Nicky then pulled out a box from his closet that had a supernatural white glow to it.

He said to me, "John, I am retiring; these are all the sermons I ever preached, and I want you to have them."

I said, "Oh, Nicky, I can't have them. You paid the ultimate price, and those are for you, a blessing from the Lord."

He came back and said, "No, John, from the bottom of my heart, I want you to have these."

So I said, "Nicky, I am beyond words. Thank you so much for this blessing."

Then I asked him if I could step into his kitchen and get a glass of water.

He said, "Absolutely."

At this point in the dream, the picture changed drastically.

As I went to the kitchen to get the water, a man was standing there who was so evil and demonically possessed that his eyes were on fire. He was wearing demonic beaded necklaces around his neck.

I looked him straight in the face, and a dark, questioning thought rose in my mind: "Is Nicky quitting Jesus and being recruited to the occult?"

At that moment I snapped out of my dream.

A couple of days later, I was talking to a pastor friend of mine and shared the dream with her to see if she could interpret it because she had a prophetic gift.

But going to her for counsel got me in trouble with the Lord!

The Lord said to me, *Didn't you ask Me to explain your calling to you? Why would you go to someone else?*

I repented of that mistake, and God spoke to me. He gave me the prophetic interpretation of the dream: He was calling me to be an evangelist.

In the dream, Nicky represented evangelism. The box that was supernaturally glowing symbolized all the sermons God would give me to preach the Gospel. The man in the kitchen who was possessed represented people who were trapped in the occult and people in the Church who were trapped with demonic demons.

The Lord said that I would be preaching the Word of God to them.

I have conquered my dream. Today I am an evangelist for Jesus Christ with no regrets. I am thankful and grateful for the calling He placed upon my life. Thank You, Jesus! Amen.

15

He Who Does Not Fight Is Doomed

In the Christian camp, the number-one thing I hear believers say is that they are waiting on God—when the battle started six months ago. Now we find ourselves late to the fight, and we cannot blame God, because the instructions were released from heaven six months prior, but we sat on our hands and sat on our anointing. The other school of thought I hear in the Church—and even from leaders—is that "we shouldn't talk about the devil because we give him glory."

That is hogwash. That is a fear demon on them because we love talking about the enemy, but very few confront the enemy. We have taken this laid-back posture: "If the enemy doesn't mess with me, then I don't have to mess with him."

The Lord Jesus Christ makes it clear that we should engage the forces of darkness and expose their deeds. King David said, "Praise be to the LORD my Rock, who trains my hands for war, my fingers for battle" (Psalm 144:1 NIV). At no moment do you hear David say, "Lord, teach me how to sit on my hands" or "Lord, teach me how to run from the devil and fight another day."

As I shared before, either you are on a cruise ship of a ministry or you are in a battleship ready to be armed and dangerous to fight the good fight of faith. Either we engage the forces of darkness or we lie down and die spiritually and discredit the name of our Lord Jesus Christ.

By no means is this chapter about fighting people or hurting anyone physically. Look again at Ephesians 6:12 (NIV): "For our struggle is not against flesh and blood, but against the rulers, against the authorities, against the powers of this dark world and against the spiritual forces of evil in the heavenly realms."

Never misjudge the enemy of your soul. We would be totally ignorant as believers not to know anything about the devil.

"Why, John?" people ask. "This is for the religious people who are fighting the darkness who always have something to say." He who lacks knowledge about the evil one will find himself sitting in the place of defeat where bondage, strongholds and misery live. Don't you know that Satan is a master and has a Ph.D. in warfare?

Throughout the history of the Bible, he set up and entrapped many—like Samson, like King David in the moments he committed murder and adultery. And Adam and Eve, and the church of Moses (the Israelites) with three million people, when they were supposed to be on a journey for eleven days to reach the Promised Land but it took forty years. And Peter, who denied Jesus three times; Judas, who sat and ate with Jesus and walked with Him for three years—and then betrayed Him.

None of these things happened because God was weak— let's get that straight. This will never be. Instead, the vessels underestimated their opponents and the seasons they were in. Remember, the devil has been fighting since he was cast out of heaven. He is very effective with his schemes, wiles and entrapments. He has a very established kingdom and system. For one thing, he gathers information against those who are trying to attack his kingdom, and then he prepares for the attack. He also loves to exploit our weaknesses with his demonic agents that do his bidding against us. They gather the demonic intelligence and use it against us, trying to take advantage of us.

Read 2 Corinthians 2:11 (NIV) again: "In order that Satan might not outwit us. For we are not unaware of his schemes."

He uses this advantage by attacking you in your dreams, in your body and in your mind. His weapons are worry, fear, anxiety, sorrow, emptiness, misery, confusion and many others. These wicked spirits know how to invade the blueprint of the season you are in and the one that you are going into.

It is time for us to be strong in the Lord and stop playing patty-cake and negotiating games with the devil. Stand in the righteousness of Christ and His holiness and make it a lifestyle. When these devils with their demonic powers try to manipulate or control you, either you fight back or suffer the spiritual consequences.

Get Your Heavenly Game Plan On

We need to get our game plan in motion by the power of the Holy Spirit and fight back. My mission here is to equip you with the arsenals of heaven so you can conquer your victory and deliverance. Here are the steps of our heavenly game plan.

Identify Who/What You Are Fighting Against

What is coming against you? Another way to word this is, What is the attack? Is it sickness, is it generational, is it witchcraft or is it a door that you opened consciously or unconsciously?

Know the Truth

John 8:32 (NIV) says, "Then you will know the truth, and the truth will set you free." Never fight the devil with your own understanding, your own theology and reasoning, or your own emotions and frail little mind-set. You fight the devil with the Word of God as Jesus did in the wilderness when the enemy tried to tempt Him three times. Think about this: Jesus was fasting and hungry; He was weak in His humanity, yet with the Word of God, He beat the devil down like Charlie Brown. The Lord Jesus Christ promised us that we can do the same thing.

Learn How to Pray Violent Fire Prayers

If you are not fearless, unmovable and untouchable when you pray, the tormentors will get the best of you. If you get spiritually violent on them by being a fearless spiritual gangster—bringing the judgments of God upon them without blinking an eye—the devil and his cronies will know you mean business. We can learn from King David and the book of Psalms.

Engage in the Warfare of Violence

We know that Satan is a thief, and he is trying to steal everything about you and me and who we are in Christ Jesus. So we need to be armed and dangerous and engage in the ministry of violence to bring destruction and conflict into the devil's kingdom by force to frustrate his evil plans against us.

Do Not Be Afraid

Fear is the biggest weapon in the enemy's camp against the believer. Fear will paralyze you and torment you.

First John 4:18 (NIV) tells us, "There is no fear in love. But perfect love drives out fear, because fear has to do with punishment. The one who fears is not made perfect in love."

The devil and his loser demons can smell fear when you walk by him the same way a dog can; the dog senses that you fear him and then he tries to attack you. Many believers lose the battle because they get demonized and tormented by fear and never stand on the offense of the fight.

Start Fasting

Jesus said, "This kind does not go out except by prayer and fasting" (Matthew 17:21 NASB1995). In the name of Jesus, Satan's power must be destroyed. Isaiah 61:1 says, "The Spirit of the Sovereign LORD is on me, because the LORD has anointed me to proclaim good news to the poor. He has sent me to bind up the brokenhearted, to proclaim freedom for the captives and release from darkness for the prisoners" (NIV).

Even the awesome apostle Paul fasted for three days before he started his ministry (see Acts 9:9). Even the beloved Daniel, our brother in Christ, engaged in spiritual warfare while fasting for 21 days.

In the third year of Cyrus king of Persia, a revelation was given to Daniel (who was called Belteshazzar). Its message was true and it concerned a great war. The understanding of the message came to him in a vision.

At that time I, Daniel, mourned for three weeks. I ate no choice food; no meat or wine touched my lips; and I used no lotions at all until the three weeks were over.

On the twenty-fourth day of the first month, as I was standing on the bank of the great river, the Tigris, I looked up and there before me was a man dressed in linen, with a belt of fine gold from Uphaz around his waist. His body was like topaz, his face like lightning, his eyes like flaming torches, his arms and legs like the gleam of burnished bronze, and his voice like the sound of a multitude.

I, Daniel, was the only one who saw the vision; those who were with me did not see it, but such terror overwhelmed them that they fled and hid themselves. So I was left alone, gazing at this great vision; I had no strength left, my face turned deathly pale and I was helpless. Then I heard him speaking, and as I listened to him, I fell into a deep sleep, my face to the ground.

A hand touched me and set me trembling on my hands and knees. He said, "Daniel, you who are highly esteemed, consider carefully the words I am about to speak to you, and stand up, for I have now been sent to you." And when he said this to me, I stood up trembling.

Then he continued, "Do not be afraid, Daniel. Since the first day that you set your mind to gain understanding and to humble yourself before your God, your words were heard, and I have come in response to them. But the prince of the Persian kingdom resisted me twenty-one days. Then Michael, one of the chief princes, came to help me, because I was detained there with the king of Persia."

Daniel 10:1–13 NIV

We must see fasting as a must in order to be victorious, not only to confront but also to destroy spiritual wickedness on every level.

Live in Holiness

Scripture says, "It is written: 'Be holy, because I am holy'" (1 Peter 1:16 NIV). Let's step into it. Psalm 24:3–5 (NIV) tells us:

Who may ascend the mountain of the LORD? Who may stand in his holy place? The one who has clean hands and a pure heart, who does not trust in an idol or swear by a false god. They will receive blessing from the LORD and vindication from God their Savior.

God understands that we will make some mistakes, but He will not tolerate a lifestyle of sin. On the other hand, the devil loves it as he knows Scripture very well: "The one who does what is sinful is of the devil, because the devil has been sinning from the beginning. The reason the Son of God appeared was to destroy the devil's work" (1 John 3:8 NIV).

Ask yourself: If you are engaging in spiritual warfare, which table are you sitting at? "You cannot drink the cup of the Lord and the cup of demons too; you cannot have a part in both the Lord's table and the table of demons" (1 Corinthians 10:21 NIV).

You can never be double-minded when you are engaging in spiritual warfare; if you are, by default you are engaging the enemy and his kingdom: "Such a person is double-minded and unstable in all they do" (James 1:8 NIV).

Listen to the Word of God over your life, over your mind and over your purpose and destiny. I declare and decree the Word of God over you now:

"We know that anyone born of God does not continue to sin; the One who was born of God keeps them safe, and the evil one cannot harm them" (1 John 5:18 NIV).

Take a moment and give God the glory, honor and praise.

16

The Atmosphere

You will never conquer your deliverance if you do not conquer and shut down your spiritual atmosphere and maintain and hold the real enforcement that comes after that. It does not matter how much deliverance you have done or how many spiritual battles you have been through. The atmosphere is a climate where demons operate and execute their plans—and where demonic climates shift and changes take place. These spiritual locations are where strategies of the dark side are made or born spiritually and where the demonic forces live, operate and manifest in the spiritual realm.

These satanic atmospheres are where the demonic attacks, strongholds and bondages coming against you take place before they manifest in the natural. As a devil worshiper, I was trained to control and operate in those diabolical atmospheres so people would never be able to conquer their deliverance. I operated from the first and second heavens, all the way down to the territory, controlling and manipulating tormenting spirits— the same tormenting spirits that torment the Body of Christ today, leaving believers struggling to find a way out. In my old life, I knew how to run in the spiritual and lock down the atmosphere over a person, that person's family, ministry, purpose and destiny.

It was all too easy to shut these things down, even if you got some deliverance. The key was that you were not able to *conquer* your deliverance. I would do things to create chaos in that atmosphere of your identity, character, personality and walk with Christ, and they were things you were not ready for and never saw coming your way.

You would find yourself lost and in trouble, trying to find your way out. This is why the Word of the Lord says we should live in the Spirit and not in the flesh, in the world or in other people's opinions: "You are of God, little children, and have overcome them, because He who is in you is greater than he who is in the world" (1 John 4:4 NKJV).

My beloved brother and sister, know one thing and one thing only—and you have to believe this and live in it: To conquer your deliverance, you need to speak and take over your atmosphere. The Word of the Lord says, "I can do all things through Christ who strengthens me" (Philippians 4:13 NKJV).

It is time to get out of the demonic climate the enemy has created over your life, your purpose, your destiny, your family, your loved ones and your ministry. I live in New York City, and if I were to get into my car and take a trip to Florida, it would probably take me eighteen to 24 hours to arrive. If I decided to go to JFK or LGA airport, however, and hop on a plane, it would take me only two hours to reach Florida. Just so, there are latitudes and altitudes in the spiritual realm. It is time to go higher. The higher I go with the Holy Spirit, the more I am able to take over the atmosphere of the enemy of my soul. We need to go higher in the battle and not fight the enemy with yesterday's arsenals.

What Is the Name of Your Atmosphere?

These are the climates where the devil and his demons live, and there are satanic weather patterns, entrapments, setups. There are open satanic doors of fear, worry, unbelief, anxiety, sickness, doubt, oppression, depression and suicide, to name a few. What is the name of your atmosphere? You can be victorious. God has given you an incredible opportunity to shame the enemy and his turf. In your atmosphere, the Lord needs to be praised and worshiped, because when you establish this in the spirit realm, it is not just a song; it is changing the climate over your life.

Why does that happen, you ask? Because when worship goes up, glory comes down.

We are used to singing songs, but we are singing nothing because the enemy has cluttered our minds—at the moment of worship—with distractions or thoughts or cares of this world. We miss the praise and worship that is due to His name because we are spiritually distracted. When I read the Old Testament as a young believer, I was shocked and blown away by how the "God system" operated when it was time for battle. I thought God would send out the best men who were fit for the fight in the battlefield. But it was like an oxymoron instead: The worshipers would go out to the battlefield first because there was something in their worship, praise and songs that *changed* the spiritual-warfare climate (the atmosphere) and weakened and confused their enemies before they engaged in the battle.

It was so amazing for me to see that because in the devil's kingdom we would engage in the battle and then sing songs later. We had some victories, but not all the time.

I say this with a broken heart: We as believers will never be able to take back what the enemy has stolen until we change our atmosphere through praise and worship. When we do that, we can exercise the authority God has given us to have full

145

control. The enemy knows where your victory is, and it is in your praise and worship.

For many, many believers today, the enemy has stolen the praise due to God. Psalm 22:3 (NKJV) says, "But You are holy, enthroned in the praises of Israel."

God Does Not Want Microwave Worship

When was the last time you truly worshiped and praised the Lord from a place of gratitude? From the depths of your soul? God does not want microwave praise and worship or lip service. It does not move anything in His heart, and it will never change the atmosphere and the dark cloud over your life, or the oppression the enemy is using as a spiritual straitjacket. I want to illustrate with an example from King David's life and testimony.

As we know the story, King David was sent by his father to take lunch to his brothers and find out how the Israelites' battle with the Philistines was going. When he got there, he found all the Israelite warriors cowering in fear because of a giant named Goliath, who hurled insults against the name of the Lord God. David told the Israelite king, Saul, that he was willing to go up against this brute.

> Then David said to the Philistine, "You come to me with a sword, with a spear, and with a javelin. But I come to you in the name of the LORD of hosts, the God of the armies of Israel, whom you have defied. This day the LORD will deliver you into my hand, and I will strike you and take your head from you. And this day I will give the carcasses of the camp of the Philistines to the birds of the air and the wild beasts of the earth, that all the earth may know that there is a God in Israel. Then all this assembly shall know that the LORD does not save with sword and spear; for the battle is the LORD's, and He will give you into our hands." . . .

146

Then David put his hand in his bag and took out a stone; and he slung it and struck the Philistine in his forehead, so that the stone sank into his forehead, and he fell on his face to the earth. So David prevailed over the Philistine with a sling and a stone, and struck the Philistine and killed him. . . . Therefore David ran and stood over the Philistine, took [Goliath's] sword and drew it out of its sheath and killed him, and cut off his head with it.

1 Samuel 17:45–47, 49–51 NKJV

What a powerful testimony of how David praised and worshiped God by his actions, the same as Abraham did when he laid Isaac on the altar in obedience to God. What are you telling your Goliath and the devils you are facing on your battlefield? As David walked into the camp, the Israelites were terrified and the atmosphere was gloom and doom. David took over the atmosphere and shut down the devil's camp that day.

Our God is a speaking God. We read in the book of Genesis that He spoke to the chaos and darkness when the earth was empty, void and dark. Chaos was everywhere. By the power of His words, He spoke creation into existence and took the dark atmosphere and dressed it up into something beautiful and very good. We as the Church of Jesus Christ are the replica of who He is on the earth.

Who has stolen the atmosphere of your words?

Proverbs 18:21 (NKJV) says, "Death and life are in the power of the tongue, and those who love it will eat its fruit."

Get Out of the Hog Pen

It is time to get up from the hog pen of the atmosphere you are in and be like the prodigal son as he came to himself. Whatever your situation, condition or dilemma, praise and worship will move the heart of God today, and you will conquer your deliverance.

The prodigal son was in a bad place, spiritually, emotionally and mentally. It was gloom and doom on every side, but the Bible says he came to himself, and the devil could not hold him down; the demons could not control him anymore. Even the pigs in the hog pen could not stop him from doing a 180-degree turn that day. His whole atmosphere was changed by one thought: *I am going back to my father's house. The game is over for the devil.* Let this be your story, not only to get your deliverance, but to conquer it once and for all.

Let me share a story with you. When the devil came at me with everything he had during my first thirty days as a believer, there are no words to describe what took place in my one-bedroom apartment at night. We are talking sheer torment. Some days I was fortunate enough to sleep during the day, and as the sun went down, I would pray for it to go back up because I knew what was waiting for me at night. The tormentors came to kill, steal and destroy. Some nights it felt as though it was never going to end, and that I would never see a sunrise again. But praise be to God, after thirty days the atmosphere shifted to my victory.

Fast-forward to when the devil took my eyesight for three and a half months, and the voices of the tormentors came again. This time they were trying to take over the atmosphere of my mind. They spewed one lie after another, day and night, and said that God was not with me, that He had abandoned me, that He did not love me, and that somehow the devil still owned me from my past. As the days, weeks and months went by, the voices got louder. After three and a half months, I conquered my atmosphere through the Lord Jesus Christ.

Fast-forward again to the time when so-called believers, who called themselves Christians but were actually agents of the devil, defrauded me. These were church members; we fellowshiped, we went on men's retreats together, we shopped together, and they slept in my home. Across ten years of what was supposed to be amazing fellowship and brotherhood, an atmosphere that seemed to be godly showed itself to be purely demonic behind the scenes, behind the clouds. In the end, those I trusted and loved hijacked the atmosphere, and I lost my finances. I lost my home. I lost my reputation as a believer; they tried to tarnish it by fabricating lies in my home church. It even got to this point: I was getting a haircut one day that I could not afford. I drove to the barbershop in the Bronx, and after the haircut was finished, I stepped out to the street to see that my car had been repossessed. I took the train home that day.

In the ashes of life, with nowhere to turn but to God, the Lord Jesus Christ took over my atmosphere. The attack led me to bankruptcy court, even though I was still preaching the Gospel in the Bahamas. Never give up, and never give in. I never gave up, and I never gave in. I cried myself to sleep; no human medication was able to soothe and heal the pain of my soul. I was spiritually bleeding, with no one to comfort me or give me a word of encouragement. It felt as if the Christian world had turned its back on me.

God was the only one by my side.

The Lord is my light and my salvation—whom shall I fear? The Lord is the stronghold of my life—of whom shall I be afraid? When the wicked advance against me to devour me, it is my enemies and my foes who will stumble and fall. Though an army besiege me, my heart will not fear; though war break out against me, even then I will be confident.

One thing I ask from the Lord, this only do I seek: that I may dwell in the house of the Lord all the days of my life, to gaze on the beauty of the Lord and to seek him in his temple.

For in the day of trouble he will keep me safe in his dwelling; he will hide me in the shelter of his sacred tent and set me high upon a rock.

Then my head will be exalted above the enemies who surround me; at his sacred tent I will sacrifice with shouts of joy; I will sing and make music to the LORD.

Psalm 27:1–6 NIV

That is how I was able to conquer my atmosphere from the devil and the foes in the unmatchable name of Jesus Christ. God is no respecter of persons; He will do the same for you today.

17

What You Do Not Destroy in the Spirit Will Destroy You

As a devil worshiper, I was trained to create physical, spiritual and emotional chaos in people's lives. Through monitoring systems of the demonic, I was under contract with these demons, through ceremonies and rituals, to have the demonic powers to bring hell into people's lives. I knew how to go under the radar against believers, those who called themselves Christians, in order to get the upper hand in the spirit realm and create satanic attacks on their children, so it would manifest in the physical realm. I would create agreements in the spirit realm with certain demons to attack their homes. By those same means, I would also bring satanic dreams and would release satanic attacks upon them so they would lose their jobs.

We understand that the Bible says to protect the ear, eye and mouth gates, but I will go a step further and say to protect yourself in the physical, spiritual and emotional realms. We tend to slack off and lose the opportunity to see things in the spiritual; we wait for it to manifest in the natural. By then, it is too late.

Where There Is Smoke, There Is Fire

We are like the person who is at home and smells smoke, but ignores it. The person only reacts when the house is ablaze, and it is too late. Instead of taking action at the first warning, we wait to see something in the physical before we react, and many times it is too late. That is what happens to believers and their walks with the Lord. The alarms in the spirit realm are sounding, but we fail to hear them. Through satanic monitoring systems with our names on them, the devil has already created something against our homes, our marriages, our children, our careers, our ministries. We have the opportunity to stop it before it starts, but we do nothing.

It is time to do something about it.

The armed forces of the military depend on devices that monitor the enemy in battle. Just so, the devil knows how to be effective against you and me; he must implement various systems to watch our every move. He studies our body language every day, our conversations, decisions, weaknesses, our prayer lives, and our walk with the Lord Jesus Christ so the demons and his kingdom can be effective and powerful against us. We must bring havoc against the powers of darkness and destruction upon every demon and monitoring system of the satanic world.

Prayers to Disable Satanic Monitoring Systems

The Holy Spirit is going before us with these powerful fire prayers. Pray them with me:

> *Father, I thank You that You have empowered me with the Holy Spirit to take action, in Jesus' name.*
>
> *Holy Spirit, take over this prayer and bring destruction against the forces of darkness, in the name of Jesus Christ.*

I pick up the sword of the Lord and shut down and cut into pieces every satanic monitoring system against me now, in Jesus' name.

Let the eyes of every evil spirit, witch and warlock that is trying to invade my life by monitoring me be plucked out, in Jesus' name.

I command all satanic systems, in the first and second heavens, to be destroyed by the fire of the Holy Spirit, in Jesus' name.

I confuse all satanic airways and frequencies that are trying to monitor me now, in Jesus' name.

Every demon that is following me die, in Jesus' name.

Every satanic security system be destroyed, in Jesus' name.

I delete my name, my family, my business and my ministry from every satanic system, with the blood of Jesus Christ now, in Jesus' name.

Arsenal Prayers for Children

Remember once again: The Bible says that "the thief comes only to steal and kill and destroy; [Jesus has] come that [we] may have life, and have it to the full" (John 10:10 NIV).

Satan's game plan against you is to destroy everything that is connected to you and your bloodline. If he cannot get you directly, he will go after your children—all the children you cherish and pray for whether they are your biological children or not. We know the devil never plays fair and hits below the belt in the fight. He wants children to rebel at the authority of the home. He wants to bring them into negative relationships outside of the house and create an environment for them that will get them hooked on drugs, alcohol and sexual immorality. He will try to destroy their minds and their thinking so they will

153

not be effective in their education. His game plan is to destroy their relationships with Jesus Christ. It is so important to know the schemes and wiles, the setups and entrapments, of the devil against your children, so you can stop him in his tracks.

> Children are a heritage from the LORD, offspring a reward from him. Like arrows in the hands of a warrior are children born in one's youth. Blessed is the man whose quiver is full of them. They will not be put to shame when they contend with their opponents in court.
>
> Psalm 127:3–5 NIV

Pray these prayers:

Father, in the name of Jesus, I dedicate my children to You all the days of their lives.

I dip all my children in the blood of Jesus.

I dip all my children in the fire of the Holy Spirit.

Let all satanic manipulation and mind control devils die now, in Jesus' name.

Let every demonic setup against my children catch on fire, in Jesus' name.

Father, I put all my children in the right hand of the Father, and no demon will be able to touch them, in Jesus' name.

I destroy all satanic programs and devices against my children now, in Jesus' name.

Every evil spirit in operation through Facebook, YouTube, Twitter, Instagram and TikTok, and all social media devices, be destroyed by the blood of Jesus Christ now.

I rebuke all satanic powers of rebellion against my children; let those powers burn up by the power of the Holy Spirit now.

> *I cancel by the fire of the Holy Spirit every satanic birth certificate and all satanic adoptions that are trying to claim my children, in Jesus' name.*
>
> *I declare and decree that all my children will be successful in everything that God has for them in their lifetimes, in Jesus' name.*

Fire Prayers for Your Home

It is time to drive demons out of your home.

Have you ever sat down and wondered where a particular sickness came from—or an argument, or confusion in a relationship, or chaos in your home—but you can never put your finger on it?

It is time to drive these devils out and get violent on them with these powerful prayers. Come into agreement for your home, as there is power in agreement and unity. It is time to regroup against these forces of darkness that are trying to run you out of your home, destroy your marriage, shipwreck your children and frustrate your decisions. Put a stop to it once and for all:

> *Devil, listen to me, I serve you an eviction notice out of my home now, in Jesus' name.*
>
> *I command all satanic forces living in my house to leave now, in Jesus' name.*
>
> *Spirits of the night that are trying to bring chaos into my home, my sleep and my dreams, burn by the fire of God, in Jesus' name.*
>
> *Spirit of divorce and every argument devil in my house, I destroy your powers now, in Jesus' name.*
>
> *Let every demonic power that has been targeting my home die now, in Jesus' name.*

Let every accusing devil that is trying to destroy my family die now, in the name of Jesus.

I call on the peace of God to rule and reign in my home, in Jesus' name.

I wash my home in the blood of Jesus.

I cover my family in the blood of Jesus.

Let the foundation of my home be purified by the fire of the Holy Spirit, in Jesus' name.

I rededicate my home, marriage, children, job and ministry back to Jesus now.

As the blood of the Passover lamb protected the people in Egypt from the angel of death, let the blood of Jesus protect my home now, in Jesus' name.

It is time to arrest every demon in the spiritual, physical and emotional realms. These demons are very bold, and if we show any signs of weakness against them, we will lose the battle. They run in groups. Know this: As believers, we are enlisted in the army of the Lord. It is time to put these demons in cages and lock them up because they are arrested in the spiritual, physical and emotional realms. They cannot work in these spiritual environments anymore.

Understand in the Spirit these words: "Finally, be strong in the Lord and in his mighty power" (Ephesians 6:10 NIV).

Declare these words of Scripture now:

All of us also lived among them at one time, gratifying the cravings of our flesh and following its desires and thoughts. Like the rest, we were by nature deserving of wrath. But because of his great love for us, God, who is rich in mercy, made us alive with Christ.

Ephesians 2:3–5 NIV

Violent Prayer Points

Father, I pick up my weapons of warfare and stand covered by the power of the Holy Spirit in this battle.

I release angels from Michael's quarters to come down and assist me in the battlefield against every demon that is trying to arrest my life, in Jesus' name.

I cover myself, my family and my home in the blood of Jesus Christ.

Lord Jesus, hide me against every satanic arrestor spirit, in Jesus' name.

I destroy all powers of satanic arrestors that are trying to arrest me in the physical, spiritual and emotional realms; let them be destroyed, in Jesus' name.

I rebuke and bind all astral-projecting demons that have been released to steal my blessing, in Jesus' name.

I destroy every astral-projecting demon that is trying to arrest me, in Jesus' name.

I burn up by the power of the Holy Spirit all satanic authority that is trying to come against me in the physical, spiritual and emotional realms, in Jesus' name.

I cut and destroy all their assignments, in Jesus' name.

May the Holy Spirit arrest them all, in Jesus' name.

I call the fire of God to fall upon every demon's head that is working against me and my family, my finances and my ministry. Let them burn now, in Jesus' name.

Take a moment and give God glory and praise for your victory!

18

Make an Assessment of Spiritual Damages

We are living in a society where the Church is more concerned about protocol than about God's people. Don't get me wrong. I respect protocol in the Church and believe we should have it. We have this thing on Sunday where we go to church and start with worship, a few announcements, the preaching of God's Word, making an altar call, then running to the parking lot to get into our cars. This is like a hamster on a wheel who thinks he is moving forward and making progress. He jumps on the wheel going 90 mph and gets off, and somehow in his mind he believes he accomplished something. We find ourselves in the same place as the Church, in fear of breaking out of the Sunday ritual. The devil sits and laughs and is waiting outside the doors of the churches to resume his attacks and torment God's people. The ministers never stop and ask the Holy Spirit what He wants to do that day.

The Great Pretenders

We come to church fragmented, spiritually distorted and falling apart, and we are afraid to tell the truth of our spiritual condition. Many Christians today are discouraged and tormented beyond the point of no return. They are filled with despair and lack of hope. We in the Body of Christ are the great pretenders today.

We ask a fellow believer, "How are you doing?"

Instead of telling the truth, he answers, "Praise God, I'm blessed."

The Church has become a masquerade party, masquerading our spiritual condition with shouts of hallelujah while we are waiting on God for a miracle. I say these things as a minister of the Gospel, and I am not afraid of criticism, because whatever the Holy Spirit wants me to say, I am going to say it. You see, I love my brothers and sisters; I am my brother's keeper. Sadly, a lot of ministers out there love the crowd but hate the people. All they care about are the finances of the church and how many members they have. No one is making any assessment of spiritual damages, asking the Holy Spirit, "What should we do?" or letting the Holy Spirit lead on Sunday instead of our traditions and formats.

Beloved, this is the real condition of the Church. We have to stop the bleeding. It is time to deliver God's people by the power of the Holy Spirit. Let's take a page from the lives of Moses, Joseph, King David and Esther. They were anointed to deliver God's people. What has happened to us today?

Let me share with you the *true* condition of the Church. Whether our brothers and sisters are battling generational curses, or have opened doors known or unknown, or have slipped away from God's perfect will, or have made a mistake by taking the wrong turn somewhere, one thing I know is that God's people love God. His people are genuine Christians at heart.

Scripture makes this clear:

> I am convinced that neither death nor life, neither angels nor demons, neither the present nor the future, nor any powers, neither height nor depth, nor anything else in all creation, will be able to separate us from the love of God that is in Christ Jesus our Lord.
>
> Romans 8:38–39 NIV

It is time to end the spiritual damages once and for all.

Beloved, please let me share with you what will expose the enemy so that when you get back in the battlefield, there will be no or very little spiritual damages in the fight. Understand that the most powerful tools you have right now—outside of the name of Jesus—are your body and mind. The devil is fighting you in your mind. He does not have to tie you up or kidnap you; he just needs to hijack your mind.

Ask Adam and Eve, who lost the precious opportunity to be in God's presence in the cool of the day. Ask Cain, who murdered his brother. Ask Esau, who lost his birthright. Ask David, when fear made him run into the Philistines' camp, and he took six hundred people with him.

> David thought to himself, "One of these days I will be destroyed by the hand of Saul. The best thing I can do is to escape to the land of the Philistines. Then Saul will give up searching for me anywhere in Israel, and I will slip out of his hand."
>
> 1 Samuel 27:1–2 NIV

A Head Checkup

Who is occupying your mind?

Stop and ask yourself this question and be honest with your answer. Let's do a head checkup. Some of the devil's tools are

- stress
- aggravation
- worry
- fear
- discouragement
- anger
- low self-esteem and
- rebellion.

These satanic arrows will make you physically sick because now your mind is sick. Lay your hands on your head right now and repeat after me:

Lord, give me a new mind. A new mind means a new perspective and new thinking. Give me a new way of looking at things. Jesus, give me a new way so I can see You and see a new way out of my situation. Lord, get my mind ready because I am coming out of my rough areas of thinking and reasoning.

My brother and sister, you are going to make it, and you are going to be armed and dangerous. Close the door in the devil's face and on the spiritual damages. The Word of the Lord says that the engrafted Word of God heals the mind. The Word of the Lord says that it is with the mind that we serve Him. Speak this over your life now so you can receive God's opportunities, put the devil on notice and destroy all spiritual damage that has been done to your life:

Do not conform to the pattern of this world, but be transformed by the renewing of your mind. Then you will be able to test and approve what God's will is—his good, pleasing and perfect will.

Romans 12:2 NIV

Trust God always in the battle. Whatever your challenges and struggles might be, the Word of the Lord says, "I can do all this through him who gives me strength" (Philippians 4:13 NIV).

Let me share one last thought with you before we close this chapter. If you do not beat the devil in your mind, you will never beat him in the battlefield of your life. We have been trying to beat the devil in the battlefield when he has already incarcerated our minds and thoughts. It is time to reverse the tables and beat him in your mind, as he is already defeated in the battlefield.

Say this last thing with me:

I am not wasting another moment, another opportunity that God gives me, and I am not wasting another year of my life. I will rise up from the spiritual damages once and for all, in Jesus' mighty, precious name. Amen.

19

How to Get Your Fight Back

I want to be transparent with you today. Many times in my walk with the Lord, I have allowed the enemy to grip me along with the circumstances in my life. It has been a challenge, and there have been many times when I have felt as though there would not be a tomorrow. The fight has been fierce. At times I felt like the apostle Paul:

> We are hard-pressed on every side, yet not crushed; we are perplexed, but not in despair; persecuted, but not forsaken; struck down, but not destroyed—always carrying about in the body the dying of the Lord Jesus, that the life of Jesus also may be manifested in our body.
>
> 2 Corinthians 4:8–10 NKJV

Every believer will go through a dark night and a dark season. The Word of God is like the oxygen of your spiritual lungs that will keep you breathing until you get to the other side. There have been many nights and mornings I have gotten up in despair, discouragement, emptiness and torment in the mind and soul. But I hang my hat on one Scripture in my life, and I repeat it for you here: "I can do all things through Christ who strengthens me" (Philippians 4:13 NKJV).

One thing I know is that I will not give up, and I will never give in. One of my Old Testament heroes of the faith is Elijah. Look at how the Lord built him up when he was at a low point:

Now Ahab told Jezebel all that Elijah had done, and how he had killed all the prophets with the sword. Then Jezebel sent a messenger to Elijah, saying, "So may the gods do to me and even more, if I do not make your life as the life of one of them by tomorrow about this time." And he was afraid and arose and ran for his life and came to Beersheba, which belongs to Judah, and left his servant there. But he himself went a day's journey into the wilderness, and came and sat down under a juniper tree; and he requested for himself that he might die, and said, "It is enough; now, O LORD, take my life, for I am not better than my fathers." He lay down and slept under a juniper tree; and behold, there was an angel touching him, and he said to him, "Arise, eat." Then he looked and behold, there was at his head a bread cake baked on hot stones, and a jar of water. So he ate and drank and lay down again. The angel of the LORD came again a second time and touched him and said, "Arise, eat, because the journey is too great for you." So he arose and ate and drank, and went in the strength of that food forty days and forty nights to Horeb, the mountain of God.

Then he came there to a cave and lodged there; and behold, the word of the LORD came to him, and He said to him, "What are you doing here, Elijah?" He said, "I have been very zealous for the LORD, the God of hosts; for the sons of Israel have forsaken Your covenant, torn down Your altars and killed Your prophets with the sword. And I alone am left; and they seek my life, to take it away."

So He said, "Go forth and stand on the mountain before the LORD." And behold, the LORD was passing by! And a great and strong wind was rending the mountains and breaking in pieces the rocks before the LORD; but the LORD was not in the wind. And after the wind an earthquake, but the LORD was not in the earthquake. After the earthquake a fire, but the LORD was not in the fire; and after the fire a sound of a gentle blowing. When Elijah heard it, he wrapped his face in his mantle and went out and stood in the entrance of the cave. And behold, a voice came to him and said, "What are you doing here, Elijah?"

1 Kings 19:1–13 NASB1995

What an awesome story in the Word of God! And what a display of a man who carried the torch of victory! Let's reflect for a second on Elijah's résumé in the battlefield. This was a man who killed 450 false prophets in one day. This was a man who was able to pray and close the heavens for three and a half years, an awesome display of the power of prayer. Then he prayed and the heavens opened and rain came. Elijah outran the chariot of Ahab, and he knew the voice of God as clear as day. But one word from the devil's mouth paralyzed him with fear and sent him on the run. He was so tormented he got to the point where the only prayer he had left to the Lord was "Kill me."

What Is the Name of Your Cave?

When we allow the enemy to put us in that state and condition, we are not only running away from the devil, we are running away from God as well. How many victories has God given us in our walk with Him, and now we are hiding in the cave of despair, the cave of fear and unbelief, the cave of sickness, bondage and torment?

What is the name of your cave?

How awesome is God to send an angel to minister to Elijah, to refresh and bless him, because God was not finished with him yet, and the journey was long. It is funny how Elijah, while in the cave, heard the earthquake and the fire, but God was absent from them. Then a still, small voice showed up to reassure Elijah that God was with him. He is with us, too. God will never leave us or forsake us. That voice to Elijah was like a cup of cold water to refresh him, because the journey was not over.

The lesson of this story is, you can have a polished and victorious résumé, but in the next chapter of your life, when God wants to bring you higher . . . let me just say one thing: New levels, new devils. Through the power of the Holy Spirit, it is time to get your fight back.

What is gripping you now that you cannot shake off? What is the name of that Jezebel? Do you find yourself, like Elijah, wanting to quit on God? Do you want to quit on your family, your marriage, your ministry, your purpose and your destiny? Spiritual drama has taken place. You are fighting this thing, and it is still coming at you harder than before.

This is not about a fight or a spiritual-warfare moment; this is about trusting God, going to a higher place that He is trying to take you to. You are trying to stay where you are comfortable. In the book of Revelation, the Lord Jesus Christ appeared to the beloved John and asked him to come up higher because He had something to show John—and us. "After this I looked, and there before me was a door standing open in heaven. And the voice I had first heard speaking to me like a trumpet said, 'Come up here, and I will show you what must take place after this'" (Revelation 4:1 NIV).

Many times we miss the higher moments with the Lord Jesus Christ. We say to the Lord, "I am under attack. I prayed, I fasted and I did everything."

God is saying to you, as He said to Elijah: *Go back. Face and confront what you have been running away from, and I will meet you there.*

Get back your fight. God has a plan for what is in front of you. It is time to shut down the voice of the enemy and his game plan against your life. It is time to obey God.

The way to get your fight back is not only by praying, fasting and going to church. These things are good and commendable, and they are a way to get your rhythm back until you see Jesus in the fight. I am talking to leaders right now. Satan has managed to get the Church off the message of the certainty of Christ Jesus. Satan's mission is nothing more than to turn God's people away from the true Gospel message. Once you are off the truth of who Jesus Christ is, bitterness and resentment enter in, and instead of living in peace with the Holy Spirit and allowing Him to work in and through you, you will end up with a disturbed spirit. You will never enter into God's promises or His rest that way. Jesus must remain center in your heart, mind and soul.

All of us around the world see the Body of Christ under severe attack, not because God is not powerful—He is all-powerful— but because we need to get our fight back. When we get our fight back, no matter what we are going through, we will see Jesus in all our present trials, standing with us in our pain, our suffering and our crises. He is with us in all things. Do not look at yourself, or you will lose the fight and never get your fight back. Instead of saying ouch, you should be saying hallelujah. Know one thing and let it be real to you: Satan cannot shape or test the faith of any believer without God's permission.

God has a purpose and plan behind every trial.

I want to share something about Peter, when Jesus said to him, "Simon, Simon, Satan has asked to sift each of you like wheat" (Luke 22:31 NLT). Getting your fight back is getting your faith back. The Word makes it clear that the devil's main goal is to destroy the faith of those who love Jesus. Many times in the battle we stand on our own faith, our own reasoning, our own judgments and our own thinking, just as Elijah did when he told God that all the prophets were dead and he was the only one left.

Peter meant well when he responded to Jesus' words that night at the Last Supper. He said, "Lord, I am ready to go with You, both to prison and to death" (Luke 22:33 NKJV). This is a bold spiritual statement, but the truth is that it only represented Peter's flesh. The Bible warns: "If you think you are standing firm, be careful that you don't fall!" (1 Corinthians 10:12 NIV).

We know how the story goes when Peter was questioned about his faith later that night, after Jesus' arrest. Rather than boldly declaring his allegiance to Jesus, he denied Him and then panicked and ran for his life.

But listen to the rest of Jesus' words to Peter spoken at the Supper: "I have prayed for you, that your faith should not fail; and when you have returned to Me, strengthen your brethren" (Luke 22:32 NKJV).

This is one of the most powerful verses in the whole Bible, and God is doing the same thing for us today. The bottom line is that your home, your children, your marriage, your health, your job/career and your ministry are under attack. I am not downplaying anyone's situation—and I have good news for you: God has not forsaken you. The book of Hebrews tells us, "He Himself has said, 'I will never leave you nor forsake you'" (Hebrews 13:5 NKJV).

You Cannot Destroy What You Cannot See

It is time to get your fight back once and for all. This is how you do it. In order to get your fight back, you have to get your spiritual vision back. You cannot defeat what you cannot see in the spirit realm. These prayers will put you in a position to obtain your spiritual eyesight to see the schemes and wiles of the enemy of your soul. Ask God for spiritual vision. You cannot destroy what you cannot see in the spirit realm. You will never get your fight back without spiritual insight in the battle. Declare and decree this Scripture over yourself:

Ask, and it will be given to you; seek, and you will find; knock, and it will be opened to you. For everyone who asks receives, and he who seeks finds, and to him who knocks it will be opened. Or what man is there among you who, if his son asks for bread, will give him a stone? Or if he asks for a fish, will he give him a serpent? If you then, being evil, know how to give good gifts to your children, how much more will your Father who is in heaven give good things to those who ask Him!

Matthew 7:7–11 NKJV

There are two rhythms to getting your fight back: First get your spiritual eyes back, and then destroy what you can see.

Arsenal Prayers to Open Your Spiritual Eyes

O Lord, You are the God who reveals mysteries and secrets, in Jesus' name.

Lord Jesus, open my eyes to see what my natural eyes cannot see.

Holy Spirit, remove my spiritual blinders, in Jesus' name.

Lord Jesus, reveal unto me that which is hidden, in Jesus' name.

Lord Jesus, open my eyes to see the wiles and schemes of the enemy, in Jesus' name.

Father God, let the eyes of my understanding be enlightened, in the name of Jesus.

Lord Jesus, I put on my spiritual eyes to see the entrapment of the enemy, in Jesus' name.

Holy Spirit, unveil to me the things my eyes cannot see and my ears cannot hear in the spirit realm, in Jesus' name.

Holy Spirit, let me understand the deep things of spiritual warfare, in Jesus' name.

Holy Spirit, let the gift of revelation be activated in and through me, in Jesus' name.

Arsenal Prayers to Destroy What You Can See

Declare and decree this Scripture:

> Finally, my brethren, be strong in the Lord and in the power of His might. Put on the whole armor of God, that you may be able to stand against the wiles of the devil. For we do not wrestle against flesh and blood, but against principalities, against powers, against the rulers of the darkness of this age, against spiritual hosts of wickedness in the heavenly places. Therefore take up the whole armor of God, that you may be able to withstand in the evil day, and having done all, to stand.
>
> Ephesians 6:10–13 NKJV

Pray these prayer points in faith, and you will put the devil on the run:

Jesus, You are the miracle worker. Thank You for the anointing You place upon my life, in Jesus' name.

Father, You anointed the Lord Jesus Christ with the fire of the Holy Spirit; I ask You to anoint me now with the fire of the Holy Spirit, in Jesus' name.

Let every demonic plan against me fall to the ground and never rise again, in Jesus' name.

I destroy the arsenals of the devil with the fire of the Holy Spirit now, in Jesus' name.

I destroy every enforcement of the enemy now, in Jesus' name.

I dismantle the plans of the enemy against me, my family, my marriage, my ministry and my purpose and destiny, in Jesus' name.

I put the judgments of God upon every wicked spirit that has been assigned to slow me down in my purpose and destiny, in Jesus' name.

I curse to the root every evil scheme and wile, in Jesus' name. Let them shrivel and die.

I break and destroy every plot of the enemy against me, in Jesus' name.

I destroy every satanic rhythm of the devil that threw me off my fight, in Jesus' name.

I destroy every satanic alignment and plot against me, in Jesus' name.

I put the fire of God upon every demon's head, against every satanic setback and against every attack against me, my family, my ministry and my purpose and destiny, in Jesus' name.

Give God glory and praise for getting your fight back, in Jesus' name.

20

Spiritual Maturity

The year 2020 was an epic year in all of our lives, for everyone around the world. It was even bigger and more dramatic than 9/11 in terms of global impact. Please understand I am not diminishing the terrorists' attack that happened on September 11, 2001—it was heartbreaking. But 2020 was a year of unpredictable circumstances. Leading up to that momentous year, we heard leaders and many others jumping around talking about 2020 and 20/20 vision. I guess we missed it because the reality was far from that when COVID-19 hit. This virus affected the world in unprecedented ways. Hospitals, nursing homes, churches, ministries, jobs, careers and families—all the way up to the White House—were impacted.

Now, in 2021, as I write this, we are banking on another year thinking that things are going to change just because the calendar year changed. It is not the calendar year that needs to change; it is our spiritual attitude that needs to change. The good news is that we are motivated to pray like never before. We are facing massive challenges in our faith and spiritual foundation, whether it is 2020 or 2021. My question to you is, How is your foundation? Always remember, when it comes to the storms of life, either you are in one now, or one is headed your way, or you are coming out of one.

Matthew 5:45 (NIV) says, "He causes his sun to rise on the evil and the good, and sends rain on the righteous and the unrighteous."

Pain is inevitable, but misery is optional. We can pick and choose. I cannot control when the storms of pain will come into my life, but I can choose not to be miserable. Jesus said this:

> "Therefore everyone who hears these words of mine and puts them into practice is like a wise man who built his house on the rock. The rain came down, the streams rose, and the winds blew and beat against that house; yet it did not fall, because it had its foundation on the rock. But everyone who hears these words of mine and does not put them into practice is like a foolish man who built his house on sand. The rain came down, the streams rose, and the winds blew and beat against that house, and it fell with a great crash."
>
> Matthew 7:24–27 NIV

Jesus is telling us here that even though the storms may slam against the house—the house is you—you will be secure as long as you are grounded in Him. Are you a Sunday Christian talker, or are you built on the Word of God to stand in the face of adversity and storms that crash against your house? As I said before, we all missed it; no one saw the COVID-19 storm coming—the pandemic storm, the civil unrest storm in the streets of every city in the United States, the political drama storms . . . We need an incredible, unshakeable foundation. No one can predict when storms will come except for God. It is not about going through the storm and battle; it is about growing in it—that is what the Lord Jesus Christ wants from His Church.

Let me give you today's broadcast for the weather and the spiritual atmosphere. Today in my life, every day and all day, God reigns and the Son shines. This should be your weather and the spiritual climate of your life, too, as a believer in our Lord Jesus Christ: "When the storm has swept by, the wicked are gone, but the righteous stand firm forever" (Proverbs 10:25 NIV).

Either you are a phony Christian or you are a believer in the good, the bad and the ugly of life.

A Tale of Three Pots

There is a story told about a young lady who was going through great hardship in life. She bounced from one storm to another. One day she sat down with her father, who was a chef, and shared her heart about the things that were going on in her life one after another, nonstop.

He sat and listened to his daughter unveil her heart. After she was finished, he put three pots on top of the hot stove, filled each pot with water and brought them to a boil. As the water boiled, no words were spoken. He then put a carrot in one pot, an egg in another and ground coffee beans in the third pot.

Later he turned the stove off and said to his daughter, "What do you see?"

He pulled out the carrot, the egg and the coffee. He asked his daughter again, "What do you see?"

She looked at him perplexed. "What's your point, Dad?"

The father responded, "The carrot went in hard but came out soft, the egg went in fragile and came out hard, and the ground coffee beans came out strong and with a rich flavor."

"So what is the point of this story?" the daughter repeated.

He explained that each one faced the same temperature of the boiling water, then he added: "The carrot went in strong and relentless, and after facing the hot water, it came out soft and weak. The egg went in fragile, and after facing the same hot water, it came out hard. The ground coffee beans went in the same hot boiling water but changed the water and came out strong. When adversity knocks on your door, which one are you?"

What Is Your Spiritual Climate?

Israel fell repeatedly into spiritual decline, just as most of us do in different seasons of our lives. We forget to keep spiritual consistency in every season that we walk with the Lord. Look at this story of God's people, the Israelites:

> For the LORD brought Judah low because of Ahaz king of Israel, for he had encouraged moral decline in Judah and had been continually unfaithful to the LORD. Also Tiglath-Pileser king of Assyria came to him and distressed him, and did not assist him. For Ahaz took part of the treasures from the house of the LORD, from the house of the king, and from the leaders, and he gave it to the king of Assyria; but he did not help him. Now in the time of his distress King Ahaz became increasingly unfaithful to the LORD. This is that King Ahaz.
>
> 2 Chronicles 28:19–22 NKJV

It was not the attack the Lord was worried about with Israel, or with you and me, as God can deliver us from any attack. The Lord's concern for Israel was their spiritual condition. The same is true for us. How is our spiritual foundation? We will always have storms in our walks with the Lord. Where will you build your house, on the rock or on the sand? This whole chapter hangs on this one thought, so do not miss it: Your greatest defense against raging storms is your foundation in Christ. Storms will either expose us or make us grow.

Bitter or Better

Israel's spiritual temperature and their response determined the outcome of their battles. There are two things that either afflict you or strengthen you—the direction you take and the decision you make going into a battle or storm. Either you stay faithful to Jesus, or you become unfaithful and bitter when you come out of the storm, out of the battle. If your house is built on the rock of Jesus Christ, choose spiritual strength so you will have a spiritual life in Jesus.

Either you can choose to let affliction frustrate you, oppress you and shorten your spiritual life, or you can choose strength and come out victorious. Standing firm will make you tougher, extend your growth and make you more powerful to withstand the time of spiritual adversity. Which one are you, or which one do you want to become? Become spiritually stronger, not spiritually unfaithful. You have two spiritual buttons: faithful and unfaithful. Let the Holy Spirit push the button, not the enemy.

Do not look at the battle, but understand the battle and look within yourself to assess the walk you have with the Lord. This is how you keep spiritual focus. We do not want things to afflict us but to make us spiritually stronger. Spiritual maturity is about kicking it into gear in our walks with the Lord. Getting deliverance and *conquering* your deliverance is an amazing thing.

To keep our deliverance, we need spiritual maturity and godly character. Many believers today—including ministers—crash and burn because there is no godly character or spiritual maturity in their foundations. We get our deliverance only to find out later that we built it on the sand and not on the rock. In fact, some people never understand the foundation they are standing on until there is a battle or storm. The battle strengthens the godly, but affliction will destroy the unprepared believer.

The outcome of our spiritual-warfare battle is determined by how we walk with the Lord day in and day out. One of two things will happen—either we will be conformed to the image of Jesus Christ, or the battle, the storms, will "deform" us into something other than whom or what God called us to be. The greatest way to grow in times of adversity is to have a vibrant walk with Jesus Christ. I have seen it day after day and time after time. Two people can go through the same situation. One will come out bitter, and the other will come out better. Which one are you?

From the storms and battles of untimely deaths in our families, divorces, job losses, what is the difference between coming out bitter or coming out better? Is your foundation solid like a rock in Christ, or does it have cracks, exposing you to the devil? The godly can only get better when bad things happen because they have a choice to go deeper with God. Battles and storms will always come. Growth is optional, but I choose growth with Jesus. Strengthening comes not because of what is around me, but because of what is in me.

Let me give you your anchor in a verse that will keep you until Jesus gets back and give you the spiritual strength you need to come out in tough times: "We know that all things work together for good to them that love God, to them who are the called according to his purpose" (Romans 8:28 KJV).

The key words here are *the called according to His purpose*. Getting the victory is available to those who love God. Never allow the devil to poison you with bitterness, discouragement and unbelief. These are the enemy's arrows of affliction.

I end this section with this Scripture:

177

Then Jesus was led up by the Spirit into the wilderness to be tempted by the devil. And when He had fasted forty days and forty nights, afterward He was hungry. Now when the tempter came to Him, he said, "If You are the Son of God, command that these stones become bread."

But He answered and said, "It is written, 'Man shall not live by bread alone, but by every word that proceeds from the mouth of God.'"

Then the devil took Him up into the holy city, set Him on the pinnacle of the temple, and said to Him, "If You are the Son of God, throw Yourself down. For it is written: 'He shall give His angels charge over you,' and, 'In their hands they shall bear you up, lest you dash your foot against a stone.'"

Jesus said to him, "It is written again, 'You shall not tempt the LORD your God.'"

Again, the devil took Him up on an exceedingly high mountain, and showed Him all the kingdoms of the world and their glory. And he said to Him, "All these things I will give You if You will fall down and worship me."

Then Jesus said to him, "Away with you, Satan! For it is written, 'You shall worship the LORD your God, and Him only you shall serve.'"

Then the devil left Him, and behold, angels came and ministered to Him.

Matthew 4:1–11 NKJV

Facing the Three Temptations

I want you to catch this in your spirit. Please do not miss this. You will be armed and dangerous if you get this. In Matthew we see Jesus face the devil head on. This was Jesus' storm, His hot-water moment when He came face-to-face with the enemy, and He left the battle strong. Jesus had three temptations. Notice how powerful and diabolical these three temptations were.

They came right after Jesus was baptized. Remember God the Father had spoken to Jesus just prior to His testing in the wilderness: "Suddenly a voice came from heaven, saying, 'This is My beloved Son, in whom I am well pleased'" (Matthew 3:17 NKJV).

The Father God said these words. Now notice the first temptation of the devil: "When the tempter came to Him, he said, 'If You are the Son of God, command that these stones become bread'" (Matthew 4:3 NKJV).

The devil said, "*If* you are the Son of God." He was attacking Jesus right in the very place where God the Father had spoken to Him, trying to destroy Him with unbelief, cause Him to question what His Father had said, and put doubt and fear in His spirit. The devil was trying to afflict Jesus with those words, the same game he played back in the Garden of Eden with Adam and Eve: "Did God *really* say . . ."

But this is the dagger that Jesus put in the devil's heart, causing him to flee: Three times Jesus said, "It is written." This means it is established, which means it is immovable, unshakeable and nonnegotiable—the Word of God.

Three times Jesus went back to the Word of God, fought the devil and destroyed his game plan. A firm foundation is how you conquer your deliverance in Christ Jesus. It is written, devil, game over!

Now, if Jesus needed the Word of God to defeat the enemy, why are you trying to fight the devil without it? If you want to be strengthened and fight the number-one enemy of your soul, let's give this devil a beat-down. God's Word in your mouth is a fire that releases the judgments of God upon Satan's head. A wordless Christian is a powerless Christian—a no-victory and not-victorious Christian. This is how we do it, beloved. This is how we build an amazing foundation in Christ.

Do not worry about repairing the cracks in your armor; instead repair the cracks in your foundation. Let me give you these three arrows to put into your quiver:

- time in prayer
- fellowship time with Jesus
- time to worship Him

With these, your foundation will never be moved and never have cracks or leaks again.

The devil might rattle your house, but he will never move you from your foundation.

21

Conquering Your Spiritual Giants

When we look at the life of David, we see a shepherd boy who grew up in a home where he was not loved and not held in high regard. In the eyes of his father and brothers, David was the misfit of the family, but in the eyes of God, David was a king, about to step into his destiny and one day lead the Lord's people the same way he led those sheep on the hillsides of Judea.

Many of us can relate through our own upbringings. Sometimes we feel that we were born into the wrong family, put into the wrong neighborhood—we grow up with a low-self-esteem complex. Whether it was rejection, or someone molested or raped you, or you were abused by the hands of someone you had no control over, or you grew up in a home like mine that was filled with silent pain, I believe in my heart this was all in God's plan for you and me, from the beginning to the end of our stories.

Winning in Christ is a process. On the outside, David looked insignificant, but inside he was a king. Esther had no mother or father and no future, just like the foster kids in foster homes today who are left behind and feel that even God has forgotten them. But Esther had a queen inside of her. When we come to the Lord Jesus Christ, this is our story as well. Yet, as God is in the process of writing our stories, we decide to take the pen out of His hand and write our own stories. And, as I said earlier, we need a bunch of white-out to fix our mistakes.

Why are we crazy enough to take the pen out of the hand of the greatest Author of all creation? It is like taking the paintbrush out of Michelangelo's hands when he was painting the masterpiece in the Sistine Chapel. How much more is our Lord Jesus Christ trying to paint a masterpiece of your life! Our mistake is that we see things in parts, and the Lord sees things in whole. On our part, we tend to make permanent decisions based on temporary situations. Many of us start something and never finish it. Rather, we need to pay the price and follow through, come hell or high water. But we do not want to count the cost—the tears and struggles and pain—or even show up for the fight. Fight on regardless of the circumstances. Fight on.

Burying My Sister

Today I came back from the cemetery after burying my sister, who passed away at the age of 29 on December 31, 2020. She departed to be with the Lord at 7:09 p.m. holding the hand of my precious mom, who stood at Desiree's bedside. This is the same mother who stood by my sister's side as a baby in the crib, taking the chance of adopting her, knowing that she was born HIV positive from her natural parents. My mother knew that one day she would pay the price of my sister passing away. Throughout her short 29 years, she fought the good fight.

My sister was rushed to the hospital on Christmas night, and on December 31, she made Jesus Christ proud because

He did not make a mistake by picking her. Desiree never lost a fight. It was her time to go home to her Savior. She never gave up on God, and God never gave up on her. It was a love story to the end. She left two little girls behind, ages six and seven, and they will carry on Desiree's legacy.

Sometimes I do not know what to say about so-called Christians who give up on God. They come to the cross, but later on, they give up on God—then say with a fake smile on their faces that they used to be a Christian. What a tragic story that will be in heaven one day! I reflect on one thing today: The last time I drove into a cemetery was 21 years ago as a devil worshiper. Now, 21 years later, I went back as a believer in Christ Jesus. I felt very proud because I was escorting my sister and not trying to buy demons or perform witchcraft on people. To God be the glory on this beautiful day.

Never give up, never give up, never give up. "I can do all this through him who gives me strength" (Philippians 4:13 NIV).

Stay on Track

What is God showing you that you are afraid of? It is funny how we have big-time faith for other people, but what about you? Go see what God has for you before you give up. Stay on the journey and do not jump off. Name one thing that God has not pulled you through. Name one; the devil is a liar. I was in the deepest world of witchcraft, and God pulled me out. I was tormented by demons for thirty days, and God pulled me through. I was betrayed in the Church, and God pulled me through. I was pushed into bankruptcy, and God pulled me through. I lost my home on a short sale, and God pulled me through. My car was repossessed, and God pulled me through. I lost my eyesight in 2002, and God pulled me through. If He has not pulled you through, it is because you are currently going through the process right now.

Why would you still be here today and wake up this morning? Winners in Jesus stay in the journey, so ask yourself: Are you walking in any place of agreement with the devil?

The devil may have turned up the heat on you, but God owns the knob on the stove. The devil is the sandpaper that God is using to polish you to make you a spiritual winner. Trust me, I have seen too much in Jesus to quit now. What makes life powerful and meaningful and substantial is that God put an expiration date on it. The devil's trick is to make us believe that we will live on this earth forever. If we were to live forever, it would be sorrowful because many of us would be spiritually lazy, thinking we had forever to get it right. We would be living for the devil instead of living for God. When God asks us to do something, we choose not to do it because our mind-set is stuck in *forever*, and so we are disobedient. I have news for you: The clock is ticking. It is time for every one of us to turn with urgency. We need to stop saying this line: "I am waiting on God."

My question for you is, What if you were to die today when you could have gotten your deliverance and conquered your enemy? We die with our gifts inside us like a mother's baby dying inside of her. What a tragic situation! The only reason I keep going no matter what, even when the world is falling apart around us, and pain and suffering seem to be the topic of the day, is that I love God and trust Him.

Like Job, I could look to my right and left and feel that He is not there. Yet in his pain, Job said, "I know that my Redeemer lives. . . . [God] knows the way that I take; when He has tested me, I shall come forth as gold" (Job 19:25; 23:10 NKJV). I have been in those moments of time; even though I could not see Him in the natural, I knew He was there.

You must push for your breakthrough, like the woman with the issue of blood.

A woman in the crowd had suffered for twelve years with constant bleeding, and she could find no cure. Coming up behind Jesus, she touched the fringe of his robe. Immediately, the bleeding stopped.

"Who touched me?" Jesus asked.

Everyone denied it, and Peter said, "Master, this whole crowd is pressing up against you."

But Jesus said, "Someone deliberately touched me, for I felt healing power go out from me."

Luke 8:43–46 NLT

This woman was an incredible person. She knew in her spirit that it was not easy to push through and get her breakthrough. She knew something that day: She knew in her heart that if she touched the Master in the spirit, she would be completely healed and set free. She would be a spiritual winner.

Overcoming the Obstacles of Your Mind

Jesus Christ never promised that it would be easy. It is time to divorce your carnal mind-set and emotions and regroup now. Time has expired: "Do not boast about tomorrow, for you do not know what a day may bring" (Proverbs 27:1 NIV).

Ask yourself the ultimate question: Why are you following Jesus? It cannot be only because you are in love with Him, as He has done so much for you and me that words cannot explain. Say to Him, "Whatever it takes, I will follow You." Come into agreement with God and dishonor the devil. Walking with God is an uphill climb, not a downhill walk, to grow spiritually and to grow in purpose and move from glory to glory. Stop giving up and stop quitting in your mind. The devil is stealing your time. The Bible says to redeem your time: "[Redeem] the time, because the days are evil" (Ephesians 5:16 NKJV).

The devil knows that there is an expiration date on your purpose and destiny—it is the day you die. Now is the time to hit back and fight back. Renew your mind-set and your gift-ings: "This is why I remind you to fan into flames the spiritual gift God gave you when I laid my hands on you" (2 Timothy 1:6 NLT).

I know these are chaotic, unpredictable, uncertain times in the world today. The foundations are cracked. But "endure suffering along with me, as a good soldier of Christ Jesus. Soldiers don't get tied up in the affairs of civilian life, for then they cannot please the officer who enlisted them" (2 Timothy 2:3–4 NLT).

I am not going to let a day, a month or a year change me. I will change it through the power of the Holy Spirit. One thing I want God to do for me—and that is to keep me hungry for Jesus all the days of my life. I refuse to be dead weight for the Kingdom of Jesus Christ. I want to be like Paul and finish my race the way he did.

> I have fought the good fight, I have finished the race, and I have remained faithful. And now the prize awaits me—the crown of righteousness, which the Lord, the righteous Judge, will give me on the day of his return. And the prize is not just for me but for all who eagerly look forward to his appearing.
>
> 2 Timothy 4:7–8 NLT

Prayers to Dispatch Angelic Forces and Defeat the Enemy

From Genesis to Revelation, we see how the Lord Jesus Christ uses His angels many times to carry out His purposes to help believers on the battlefield. Angels are created beings that have supernatural strength and live in the presence of God waiting for an assignment to be dispatched and help us win the good fight of faith.

Say this prayer with me now:

Listen to me, Satan, I'm attacking you and your kingdom from my place of authority sitting with Jesus Christ in the highest of the highest heavens.

I release warring angels from Michael's quarters to fight with me in the battlefield today to destroy the works of the enemy.

Lord Jesus, You give Your angels charge over me to deliver me and my family from every satanic attack, in Jesus' name.

Let the mighty angels do war with me against the devil and his kingdom that are working against me, in Jesus' name.

I release angels of war to destroy every curse, infirmity and stronghold against me and my family, in Jesus' name.

By the power of God, I release angelic special operations forces to destroy every principality that has been assigned against me and my family, in Jesus' name.

Lord, let every angel destroy every demon that is trying to terrorize me and my family now, in Jesus' name.

Reinforcement Prayers

Repeat these reinforcement prayers with me now:

I apply the blood of Jesus over my home, my marriage, my children, my finances, my health and my purpose and destiny, in Jesus' name.

Let every evil strategy be drowned in the blood of Jesus now.

I declare a hedge of protection around me now, in Jesus' name.

187

Let every satanic operation against my purpose and destiny be destroyed now in the blood of Jesus.

I destroy the plans of the enemy that are trying to frustrate me now, in Jesus' name.

I dip myself, my family, my ministry and my purpose and destiny in the blood of Jesus Christ.

I pour the blood of Jesus over every witchcraft altar, every satanic plan against me, against my today and my tomorrow and against my family, in Jesus' name.

I seal all these prayers in the blood of Jesus and destroy all backlash of retaliation and revenge spirits of all kinds against me, my family, my ministry, my home and my purpose and destiny, in Jesus' name.

Finish by giving God the praise, glory and honor for what He has done in your life, in Jesus' name.

22

Conquering Your Season

We have the tendency to believe the devil and his lies about a new day or a new year. Why not believe God instead for a new you? It is not the ticking of your watch that brings change; God is not saying that if you pass this particular date, then all things will become new in your calendar of life or you will have His blessings. The devil wants to play us. God wants to teach us that change does not come easily.

The fake church, the house of Satan, never stops tempting believers to take up his offer of a microwave church—which promises that if we just fast for ten minutes, or drench ourselves in olive oil, or shout out loud to grab it and claim it, or practice five easy ways to our victory, or three jump-starts to a new life, then somehow we will be transformed easily and quickly.

Truth be told, the only way that we will be transformed into the likeness of Jesus Christ is if we allow the Holy Spirit to disciple us and discipline us. The Holy Spirit wants to teach you and me how to discipline our minds. He wants to remove from us the thinking of a carnal mind, which leads to carnal decisions.

189

Now that we understand what God is trying to show us and teach us, we need to stay focused on it. He wants to fortify you mentally, emotionally and spiritually to make you spiritually stronger against the onslaught of the enemy. Then when the demonic storms come, you are able to stand firm, built up into a spiritual house for Him. The Lord is not interested in church buildings; He wants to impart to you spiritual resistance against the enemy of your soul and his demons. "Therefore submit to God. Resist the devil and he will flee from you" (James 4:7 NKJV).

Stay Strong in Dark Seasons

Those times when the unexpected shows up or you cannot see the light out of a tunnel, I call dark seasons. You must stay strong in the fight mentally, spiritually and emotionally. These are gateways and portals into our inner man that the enemy is trying to break into. Through these spiritual areas, the devil is trying to take you over. If you allow the Holy Spirit to disciple and discipline you, the doors of those places will be closed, and the devil will not have legal rights over you.

Remember, the first place the enemy attacks is the mind. We cannot control the thoughts that come into our minds, but we can control the thoughts that *dwell* in our minds. Let me teach you something. We can change the colors in our houses by painting the walls, and we can change the name of our ministries—these things can be done quickly. But changing old thinking and old habits or generational things that are in us only comes through discipleship and discipline by the Holy Spirit in our lives. Conquering your season involves your thinking, your words and your spiritual actions.

Whether the devil has a stronghold in your marriage, your ministry, your job or your children, we all want transformation.

This will involve your thinking, your words and your spiritual actions. It is not about a day, month or year that brings transformation.

I see brothers and sisters year after year stuck in the same places, yet thinking they are accomplishing something. This is a lie of the devil. It is sad to see believers living their spiritual lives in this condition.

When we don't see change, we blame God, get mad at God and then leave God. Change is a 180-degree turn; it is time to turn.

The prodigal son was in the hog pen when a thought suddenly occurred to him, and he turned 180 degrees.

> "When he came to himself, he said, 'How many of my father's hired servants have bread enough and to spare, and I perish with hunger! I will arise and go to my father, and will say to him, "Father, I have sinned against heaven and before you, and I am no longer worthy to be called your son. Make me like one of your hired servants."'"
>
> "And he arose and came to his father. But when he was still a great way off, his father saw him and had compassion, and ran and fell on his neck and kissed him. And the son said to him, 'Father, I have sinned against heaven and in your sight, and am no longer worthy to be called your son.'
>
> "But the father said to his servants, 'Bring out the best robe and put it on him, and put a ring on his hand and sandals on his feet. And bring the fatted calf here and kill it, and let us eat and be merry; for this my son was dead and is alive again; he was lost and is found.' And they began to be merry."
>
> Luke 15:17–24 NKJV

So, John, how do I conquer my year or my moment—my season?

When you make that 180-degree turn, I promise you, just like the prodigal son, the Father will wait for you right down the road, and He will celebrate you. At that moment, you said no to the devil and yes to King Jesus. We think that because we took a class or read a book or listened to a sermon, somehow we are changed. Do not get me wrong; these things do help, but the spiritual reality is that we are stuck in microwave Christianity. We need the Holy Spirit to teach and disciple us at the core of who we are to bring transformation. Jesus promised: "The Helper, the Holy Spirit, whom the Father will send in My name, He will teach you all things, and bring to your remembrance all things that I said to you" (John 14:26 NKJV).

Shake Off the Enemy

It is time to finish the fight against the things that always pull us down. We need to be rooted deeper in Jesus. Hebrews 12:1 says, "Therefore we also, since we are surrounded by so great a cloud of witnesses, let us lay aside every weight, and the sin which so easily ensnares us, and let us run with endurance the race that is set before us."

Let's stop and do a spiritual assessment. Are there things that you have been fighting for days, months, years? Look again at the life of David: He had a Goliath moment, but that was not his true victory. His victory was that he ran from King Saul for thirteen years of his life. That was his battle before he became king and sat on the throne of Israel.

We should not discount any moments of victory; they are nice to have on our spiritual résumés. Look at the life of Peter. He walked with Jesus for three years; he even had a moment when he walked on water, but he later betrayed Jesus on dry land. We celebrate the one-moment victories—and there is nothing wrong with that; they should be celebrated—but the real battle, the real spiritual-warfare fight, is that one thing you know the name of. You hit it hard, but it keeps coming back to you. It is time to conquer what is in front of you and put it away once and for all.

God told Moses that the Egyptians he saw that day, he would see no more. He is saying the same thing to you, today. Like Pharaoh, the devil that has been chasing you, tormenting you and plaguing you will die today, in Jesus' name. The battles are a blessing to bring spiritual maturity. It shames and defeats the devil at his own game. One thing I want to share with you that helped me throughout the years—and I thank God for teaching me this in my spiritual-warfare fights—is to have gratitude in the battlefield. Avoid these three things: murmuring, grumbling and negative words. If you fall into doing these things, you will miss it all; repent and get back on track. The highest appreciation you can give God is not to utter words but to live by them with a spirit of gratitude.

How do you do this, John? How do you keep a spirit of gratitude in your darkest moments?

I am glad you asked. I watch my words so I do not have a negative mind-set or negative spirit and do not have a pity party. When the enemy looks as if he is winning, I do not open the spiritual doors to give him the opportunity. Look at these words of Scripture:

> Be alert and of sober mind. Your enemy the devil prowls around like a roaring lion looking for someone to devour. Resist him, standing firm in the faith, because you know that the family of believers throughout the world is undergoing the same kind of sufferings.
>
> 1 Peter 5:8–9 NIV

Always remember the goodness of the Lord in the fire, the small victories and the raindrops. When I go through my darkest times, I meditate on God's goodness in my life; I look at my spiritual résumé. I talk to myself about what looks like a defeat, but then it starts to turn around. It is like the sun bursting through the clouds.

Look at this scene from David's life: "Now David was greatly distressed, for the people spoke of stoning him, because the soul of all the people was grieved, every man for his sons and his daughters. But David strengthened himself in the LORD his God" (1 Samuel 30:6 NKJV).

As you see, when David was at his worst and lowest moment, he did something courageous. He remembered God's goodness in the battle. Even his own people wanted to kill him that day. It is always the people closest to us that the devil will use.

Build Up Your Spiritual Résumé

The life of Paul the apostle is an amazing example of someone who, through hell or high water, built a spiritual-warfare résumé.

Listen to this:

> Three times I was beaten with rods; once I was stoned; three times I was shipwrecked; a night and a day I have been in the deep; in journeys often, in perils of waters, in perils of robbers, in perils of my own countrymen, in perils of the Gentiles, in perils in the city, in perils in the wilderness, in perils in the sea, in perils among false brethren; in weariness and toil, in sleeplessness often, in hunger and thirst, in fastings often, in cold and nakedness—besides the other things, what comes upon me daily: my deep concern for all the churches.
>
> 2 Corinthians 11:25–28 NKJV

When Paul was put in jail, he and Silas worshiped the Lord, and the jail doors opened.

But at midnight Paul and Silas were praying and singing hymns to God, and the prisoners were listening to them. Suddenly there was a great earthquake, so that the foundations of the prison were shaken; and immediately all the doors were opened and everyone's chains were loosed.

Acts 16: 25–26 NKJV

Wherever the enemy has incarcerated you, those doors are about to open now, just as they did for the apostle Paul and brother Silas. You need to value who you are in Christ. It is time to grow and increase. Shame the enemy because God is with you. Look into the devil's eye, head on, and say, "It's not what you throw at me, but what I do about it."

Strengthen your position in the spirit realm by the power of the Holy Spirit. Repeat this Scripture with me:

The LORD is my light and my salvation; whom shall I fear? The LORD is the strength of my life; of whom shall I be afraid? When the wicked came against me to eat up my flesh, my enemies and foes, they stumbled and fell. Though an army may encamp against me, my heart shall not fear; though war should rise against me, in this I will be confident.

Psalm 27:1–3 NKJV

Come into agreement with God and repeat these prayers points with me; the devil and his demons will not be able to move you out of the position of strength. You will take ground back from the enemy. Get ready to open your mouth loud. It is time for war:

I declare that I am a child of God.
I decree over my life that I am born again by the Spirit of God.

195

Jesus has become the curse for me; therefore, devil, I am the righteousness of God in Christ Jesus.

I am a citizen of heaven, in Jesus' name.

I am the head and not the tail, in Jesus' name.

Devil, listen to me: I am reigning and seated with Christ in the third heaven, in Jesus' name.

Satan, your kingdom is under my feet, in Jesus' name.

I am blessed with all spiritual blessings through Christ Jesus, who gives me the strength.

Today and forever, my life is hidden in Christ.

I will, therefore, live and not die, in Jesus' name.

I renounce any weakness of my mind, spirit and soul, in Jesus' name.

I declare and decree over my mind, heart, spirit and soul that I am whole, in Jesus' name.

I curse to the root every satanic attack and the arsenals of the enemy; let them be destroyed by the blood of Jesus.

I confess that I am a man (or woman) of war, an overcomer through Jesus Christ, who gives me the strength.

Today, no weapon formed against me will prosper, and every demonic assignment will be destroyed now, in Jesus' name.

I have conquered my deliverance by the finished work of the cross, in Jesus' name.

Take a second and give God praise and glory through His Son, Jesus Christ.

23

My Story

Throughout this book, we have talked about spiritual warfare, and we know it has to do with the demonic realm, demonic attacks and facing the enemy head on. But this is not all that spiritual warfare is about. The key to spiritual warfare is this: Do we trust God in the battle? Without this, we have nothing. We can have the playbook of the enemy, we can understand how the spirit realm works, but if there is no trust in Jesus Christ, there will never be a victory.

On January 9, 2021, I held a Zoom session on mass deliverance with an amazing brother of mine, Richard Keltner, who has a ministry called Strike the Head of the Serpent. We teamed up with my longtime friend Pastor Armen of Foundation of Truth Church in California. That day, the Holy Spirit destroyed the works of the enemy. More than 140 people from around the world took part in this powerful mass deliverance session. We put a crack in the foundation of the devil's kingdom. The demons were confused, and they were all scattered from the north, south, east and west.

It felt the same as when I went to visit an awesome friend of mine in Louisiana with a powerful ministry. The day he picked me up from the airport, he heard the fearful whispers of the demons say, "John Ramirez is here, and we are in trouble. We don't know what to do. We are in trouble."

That is how I felt on January 9; the demons were in trouble. One woman on the Zoom call had a twenty-year hemorrhage issue that the doctors could not resolve. That day, the Lord Jesus Christ healed her completely and set her free. There were many other testimonies that day, one after another, and many were set free. Glory to God, and praise be to His name!

The backlash, retaliation and retribution came right after. It struck one of the people involved with the Zoom call with medical issues that required a trip to the doctor for treatment and prescriptions. What do we say to this? Is this fair?

The backlash and retribution I received in the battle came soon after: The devil struck down my eyesight once again. He knocked off my cataract lens that was permanently put into place by one of the best surgeons in New York in the early 1990s. It was such a demonic attack that even when I went to see a specialist, he said that he had never seen anything like this happen, including with all the doctors and specialists in the practice. He said it was crazy, strange and weird.

Do we say God is unfair? Allowing the backlash and revenge spirits to attack me and others on this level?

If God had asked me ahead of time—I am talking about the CEO of the universe, the One who sits on the circle of the earth—if God were to say to me, "I am going to send you into the battlefield to represent My name to bring glory to it. I want to set many people free. But this is the outcome: The devil will take your eyesight again, for a moment, and you will be blind once again. Will you still go into the battlefield and represent My name?"

My brother and sister, I ask you the same thing. Would you go, or would you reject the mission? Would you say, "Not me, Lord, pick someone else"? Or would you obey and step into the enemy's camp to the gates of hell, knowing there is a price to pay? I am at this writing losing my eyesight again, for a moment. It is one thing to be born blind and another to become blind. Would you refuse the calling? Would you chicken out? Would you shame the Lord Jesus Christ and make the devil proud because you did not want to pay the price to set the captives free?

This is what separates the saints from the "ain'ts." This is what I call those who have been set apart to become spiritual gangsters for the Kingdom of God.

So, you see, the battle is not about what we get out of it. It is about trusting God—that is the foundation of spiritual warfare and setting the captives free. In my spiritual pain, there is victory and also joy. The many who took part in the Zoom deliverance call on January 9 are not slaves to the devil anymore. The devil not only lost his grip that day, he also lost the battle.

There is no guarantee when you go into the battle that there will be any spiritual or physical wins. Listen again to the words of Job: "He knows the way that I take; when he has tested me, I shall come forth as gold" (Job 23:10 NKJV).

P.S. I am on my way to eye surgery and praying with all my heart that God will use the doctors and anoint their hands and give them the wisdom to restore my eyesight once again. Praise be to God, because I know He does not give us any more than we can handle.

One thing I have learned in spiritual warfare is to understand the rhythm of the fight and position yourself through our Lord Jesus Christ and in the power of the Holy Spirit so that you can have spiritual endurance, wisdom, knowledge and discernment to conquer your victory. This spiritual-warfare fight that I am in for my eyesight is going twelve rounds. Throughout the fight, sometimes I feel like the devil has me by the throat, and other times, I feel like I have him by the throat. I know that when it is all said and done, I will be the one standing in the name of our matchable Lord Jesus Christ. I will have my 20/20 vision, and I will conquer my victory.

Epilogue

A Letter to the Church

I am writing this letter to all who are on the brink of exhaustion, about to faint and feeling overwhelmed by your present situation. You are a faithful servant, blessing others and confident that God can do the impossible, yet you have lingering doubts about His willingness to intervene in your own struggles. I wonder how many of us have spoken words of faith and hope to others who are facing distressing and seemingly hopeless situations. You have urged others to hold on. The Lord is able, and He is a miracle-working God. His promises are true, so don't lose hope—because He is going to answer your cry.

Do you really believe in miracles? The Holy Spirit is asking you this question.

As you look back, I know you have seen the goodness of God upon your life. God wants you to remember not only the wonderful things He did for you yesterday, but also to expect His miracle-working power today. Trust Him for the things He has predestined for you in His amazing timing. God has a plan for you. I even step out in faith and call it a big plan, a perfect one.

The powers of darkness, however, do not want God-ordained destinies and purposes to be fulfilled in your life. The devil has dispatched his demon spirits and even human agents to launch a fierce attack against you and me. The enemy is strong, relentless, swift and experienced in the battlefield of your life. But there is a promise in Scripture that the gates of hell cannot prevail against the finished work of the cross. There is a name above every name, above your battles. His name is Jesus Christ. He has given us His Holy Spirit to crush the kingdom of darkness underneath our feet—yesterday, today and forevermore.

Do you believe in miracles? Think of the one difficulty and greatest need you are facing right now—the most troubling situation. I know you have prayed about it a long time. Do you really believe the Lord can work it out in ways of which you cannot conceive? That kind of faith commands the heart to quit fluttering or stop asking questions. It tells us to rest in the Father's care. Trust Him, and do it in His way and in His time. You have conquered your deliverance in the almighty name of Jesus Christ. Amen.

Prayer Manual

Prayers for Conquering Your Deliverance

My brother and my sister, please understand that before you pray these conquering prayers of deliverance, you must first be secure in Christ Jesus. In other words, not only be born again but have peace with God and believe in the finished work of the cross—that Jesus was crucified for your sins. Confess all your sins and nail them to the cross with the precious blood of Jesus Christ, the Son of God, who washed them all away.

This will start to break the legal rights of the enemy, the strongholds and bondages and his taking advantage of you. It is time to be set free once and for all and conquer your deliverance in Jesus' name.

In the mission of dealing with personal sins, ancestral sins, witchcraft, demonic soul ties, ungodly soul ties, trauma, unforgiveness and bitterness—or anything that has you bound—as you pray these prayers, you can add any additional specific name in the appropriate place so we can put the devil on notice and destroy the demonic arsenals over your life. Through the blood and name of Jesus Christ, all things are possible.

Round One

We begin by asking the Holy Spirit to anoint you. Repeat this prayer with me:

Prayer of Protection

Father God, in the name of our Lord Jesus Christ, by the power of the Holy Spirit, I proclaim the precious blood of Jesus upon myself, from the top of my head to the souls of my feet. Let the blood of Jesus Christ invade my mind, body, spirit and soul, as well as my subconscious and conscious, my thoughts, imaginations and emotions. Please take over, Holy Spirit; You are the finger of God, and You are in control of my life. Breathe into me and fill me with Your power.

Father, right now, in the name of Jesus, I call upon warring angels of heaven to come forth and surround me to bind up all demonic entities and principalities and evil spirits, in the name of our Lord and Savior, Jesus Christ, I pray, so let it be, amen.

Declare this Scripture:

Death and life are in the power of the tongue.

Proverbs 18:21 KJV

Prayer of Forgiveness

Now let's deal with the number-one enemy of unforgiveness. Repeat this prayer with me:

Father, I confess that in the past I have held unforgiveness and bitterness in my heart against certain people who have hurt and disappointed me. I recognize this as sin

204

and confess it as sin. Lord, You say in Your Word that if we confess our sins, You are faithful and just to forgive us our sins and to cleanse us of all unrighteousness. So now I forgive the following people who have hurt or disappointed me.

Say the names of the people you need to forgive now. Release forgiveness in your heart toward them. Picture them, release them and ask the Lord to heal and cover the root of unforgiveness and bitterness with the blood of Jesus Christ. Ask the Holy Spirit to break and destroy any ground of unforgiveness right now. Say this:

Now I really forgive all the people known and unknown, and I ask You, Lord Jesus Christ, to bless and save them. I also forgive myself for all my many faults and failures. Forgive me now, in Jesus' name. Please, Lord, forgive me for judging others with a wrong spirit. Release me now from any tormenting spirits that might gain access into my life, in Jesus' name.

Now say this with me:

Thank You, Father, for freeing me from the load of bitterness, unforgiveness and resentment. In Jesus' name I pray, Amen.

Confessing Contacts with the Occult

Heavenly Father, I confess to You that in the past through ignorance, curiosity or willful choice, I came into agreement with the occult and with certain occult things of the devil. I now recognize and confess these as sin and ask for forgiveness in the name of Jesus. I do confess and renounce all contacts that I made with the occult through objects, psychics and mediums with the following occult things [name them now]: Ouija boards, tarot cards, tea leaves, palm reading, witchcraft ceremonies, rituals, mediums, physics, horoscopes and contacting the dead (séances). I also renounce and confess as sin any oaths I made with any false gods, demons, idolatry of any kind and the devil and all satanic contracts. It is time to close the door in the devil's face.

Satan, I rebuke you in the name of the Lord Jesus Christ. I am closing all satanic doors that I or my ancestors opened to you and all the demons attached to those doors. I renounce Satan and all his demons; I hate them and declare them to be my enemies. I want them to leave my life now completely, in the name of the Lord Jesus Christ.

I now declare deliverance from any and all evil spirits that are in or around me. I want them out once and for all. I shut the door in my life to all occult practices and command all connections and agreements of evil spirits to leave me now. I proclaim the blood of Jesus upon my life and upon all doors, gateways and portals the enemy has had in my life.

Breaking Curses

In the name of Jesus, I break any and all curses placed against me by witchcraft spells or enchantments and command the curses and the demons to return back to the sender. I bind those curses to them by the blood of Jesus Christ.

I destroy the powers of any and all blood sacrifices and rituals invoked against me or my family, in the name of Jesus. I declare the blood of Jesus upon all personal items that the workers of the satanic world may have accumulated against me. I declare the blood of Jesus upon my hair, upon my clothing, upon photos of me and my family, upon my birthday, upon my written name, upon my signature, upon my handwriting, upon any created dolls made in my image and any other objects that have been stolen from me. I declare all of these curses to be destroyed now by the power of the blood of Jesus Christ.

I break off of myself and my family the curse of leviathan, back twenty generations on both sides of my family's bloodline, and even as far back as Adam and Eve, in the name of Jesus Christ, by His blood.

I break any curse of rejection from the womb or illegitimacy that is in my family bloodline; I break it and destroy it all the way back to the Garden of Eden on both sides of my family bloodline, in Jesus' name.

I break and loose myself from all subjection and agreements known and unknown in my family's bloodline, in Jesus' name.

I renounce and break and loose myself and my family from all demons, subjections and every ungodly soul tie, through my mother, father, grandparents or any other person, living or dead, who has ever controlled me in any way that is contrary to the will of God and His Word, in Jesus' name.

I thank the Lord for setting me free. I also repent and ask forgiveness if I have ever dominated or controlled any person in the wrong way.

Keep going; you are doing very well.

Round Two

Repeat these prayers after me:

Renunciation of Witchcraft and Psychic Bondage

In the name of the Lord Jesus Christ, by the power of His precious blood, I now renounce and break every curse and loose myself and all my descendants from all hereditary demonic strongholds of psychic powers and bondages; bonds of all physical and mental illness; and all curses that are upon me or my family's bloodline as a result of sin transgressions, iniquities, sorcery, witchcraft and all occult involvement of myself, my parents and ancestors, my family and all loved ones, right now, in the name of the Lord Jesus and the awesome power of His blood. I break off and loose myself and my family from all evil curses, incantations, chanting, charms, crystals, hexes, vexes, voodoo, burning incense candles, bewitchments, rituals and all satanic contracts of herbs, powders, oil, eggs and animal blood sacrifices. I curse them to the root in the name of Jesus, never to rise again. I free myself by the power of the Holy Spirit, in Jesus' name.

I renounce spells of death, destruction, graveyard dirt, coffins, needles, pins, sickness and every evil disease, satanic meditation, demonic dream, evil image, sorcery of every level that may be upon me or in my family bloodline of witches, warlocks, covenants that may transfer from person to person and from every level of the occult. Let it shrivel up and die now, in Jesus' name.

I declare the blood of Jesus upon these satanic powers to be void and sent back to the senders, and I cover my family and myself in the blood of Jesus Christ.

Cutting Evil Soul Ties

Father God, in the name of Jesus, I break and renounce, cut, burn and break down to the root all evil soul ties that I have with spirits of adultery and drunkenness in my mother's or father's bloodline, and with members of the occult, and also all ungodly family soul ties, relationships, ex-spouses and fornication demons—let them be destroyed and never rise again, in Jesus' name.

Heavenly Father, please unknit and cut off from my soul every ungodly soul tie right now, in Jesus' name. Please knit my soul to You by Your Holy Spirit, in Jesus' name.

Loosing the Mind

In the name of Jesus Christ, by the power of His precious blood, listen to me, devil, and all of your demons: loose my mind now of every satanic image and thought of all kinds; let those images and thoughts be destroyed with the blood of Jesus Christ. I ask You, Father, to send Your angels to loose and break and cut to the root and sever all fetters, bands, chains, cords, bonds and whatever sword the enemy may have managed to place on my mind, body, spirit and soul by words or deeds.

Father God, in the name of Jesus Christ, loose into me and my family the full power of the Holy Spirit to burn these things out of me. Let the fear of the Lord keep me by the power of His love and give me a sound mind, grace, peace and comfort. I claim it to be my victory.

Take sixty seconds and give God praise and worship for your victory.

Restoration of a Fragmented Soul

Repeat this powerful prayer with me:

Heavenly Father, I ask You in the name of Jesus to send ministering angels to gather up the fragments of my soul, to the north, south, east and west, everywhere and anywhere it is scattered. Restore my soul to the rightful place in me, because You are the lover of my soul.

Declare this Scripture over your life:

He restores my soul; He guides me in the paths of righteousness for the sake of His name.

Psalm 23:3 NASB

Repeat this prayer:

Heavenly Father, with the full power and authority of the Lord Jesus Christ to break all vessels, bands and bindings that have been put upon my soul by any means, restore all the pieces of my fragmented mind, soul, emotions, personality and character. Bring them into proper alignment now, in Jesus' name.

Confession of the Sins of the Fathers

In accordance with Leviticus 26, I do now confess my sins and the sins of my ancestors and ask for forgiveness for our sins. I petition and proclaim the blood of Jesus to be sprinkled over myself, my family, my loved ones and our purpose and destinies, and to destroy all the roots and legal grounds of these sins on both sides of my family's bloodline, back twenty generations and even as far back as Adam and Eve. All sins of idolatry, witchcraft, fornication and lust, incest, drinking blood, murder, abortion, stealing, injustices, cruelty to any persons, including family and loved ones, mistreating the poor, covetousness, occultism, divination, adultery, divorce, homosexuality, lesbianism, pedophilia, perversion, bestiality, necrophilia, necromancy, fear, rebellion, stubbornness, wicked heart of unbelief and all sins known and unknown. Let the blood of Jesus cleanse me of them. I declare forgiveness because of the provision in 1 John 1:9 (nkjv)—"If we confess our sins, He is faithful and just to forgive us our sins and to cleanse us from all unrighteousness"—and I break the cycle of recompense and lift the curse, woe, whoredoms and iniquities off of me and my descendants, in the name of Jesus. I command all spirits associated with these to leave me and my family and go to wherever Jesus wants to send them, in Jesus' name.

Prayer of Surrender to Jesus

I come to You, Lord Jesus, as my Deliverer. You know all my problems and all the things that drive, torment, defile and harass me. I loose myself from every demonic spirit, from every evil influence, from all satanic bondages and strongholds, and from every spirit in me that is not of the Spirit of God and the Father. I rebuke and command all such spirits to leave me now, in the name of Jesus Christ. I confess and declare that my body is a temple of the Holy Spirit, redeemed, cleansed and sanctified by the blood of Jesus Christ. I ask the Holy Spirit to go into my body and burn out every wicked spirit, in Jesus' name, right now. Satan, you have no place in me and no power over me because of the blood of Jesus Christ. Amen.

Exercising My Heavenly Authority

Declare and decree this over yourself:

Satan, I am seated in the heavenlies, far above you and your kingdom of powers. In the mighty name of the Lord Jesus Christ, I am positioned in Christ at the right hand of my heavenly Father, in the highest heavens. This places me high above you, your kingdom, principalities, evil spirits and every evil power, throne, dominion and world ruler. Rulers of darkness, kings and princes, and every other fallen angelic being, you are all under my feet. I command all demons to manifest out of me. Do not touch the Lord's anointed. In the name of the Lord Jesus, I ask the heavenly Father to release warring angels on my behalf to make war against all satanic forces now, in Jesus' name.

Furthermore, I command in Jesus' name that the free demonic spirits that are coming out of me now be bound and taken to where Jesus sends them and never to return. I take the authority from the highest heaven, where I am seated with Jesus Christ, and remind all evil spirits that you must obey. I command you to leave me now, in Jesus' name, and go to where the Lord sends you and never return.

Right now, in the name of the Lord Jesus Christ, and by the power of the Holy Spirit, through the precious blood of the Lamb that redeemed me, I command all foul wicked spirits to be bound and come out of me, in the name of Jesus, and I send you to the dry places.

Spirits of the occult, come out now. Ouija board, sorcery, witchcraft, mind control, Wicca, every water spirit, voodoo, divination, every Egyptian devil, fortune-telling, tea leaves, crystal ball, palm reading, astrology, horoscope and all spirits of the signs of the Zodiac, come out now, in the name of Jesus. Manifest and go; you cannot stay— you have to go now, in Jesus' name.

You're doing awesome! Let's keep going.

All spirits of hypnosis and ESP, spiritualism, mediums, séance, transcendental meditation, astral projecting, false inner healing, soul travel and mind control, come out now, in the name of Jesus. Loose me now and go, in Jesus' name. I rebuke all demons associated with the occult and any Eastern religion devils, symbols, images, burning of candles and incense—you need to come out now, in the name of Jesus, and never return.

Repeat after me:

In the name of Jesus Christ, I command all spirits of Eastern religions to manifest and go now. Hinduism, Kundalini, Tantra, Mantras, chakras, yantra, Taoism, Confucianism, I Ching, Krishna, Zen, Psi, Jehovah's Witness, Christian Science, Mormonism, Scientology, Moonies, Islam, Black Muslims and every other satanic religion, I rebuke and destroy all legal rights to me, in Jesus' name. All these spirits leave me now, in the name of the Lord Jesus Christ. Depart and go now; move, in Jesus' name.

Round Three

This is a prayer to break off ungodly practices and allegiances to the occult world. Repeat these prayers after me:

All demonic spirits of yoga, acupuncture, martial arts, Freemasonry, Eastern Star, pentagram and every fetish

*devil, enchantment, potion and spell, I rebuke you. Come
out now, in Jesus' name.*

*Every demon that came in through Harry Potter, Poké-
mon, pyramids, false vision, superstitions, Satanism,
karma or third eye, I break all the curses and contracts
made, known and unknown. Loose me now and come
out, in the name of Jesus.*

*I renounce the spirit of pride, self-hate, lowliness, de-
spair, hopelessness, hate, suicide, rejection, depression,
misery, tormenting devils, doubt, unbelief, guilt, shame
and condemnation. All these spirits, I bind and rebuke
you and command you to come out now and go to the
pits of hell, where you belong, in Jesus' name. Release me
now, in Jesus' name.*

Declare the Word of God over you right now:

God has not given us a spirit of fear, but of power and of love
and of a sound mind.

2 Timothy 1:7 NKJV

It is time to destroy the spirit of fear and be set free once
and for all. Repeat after me:

*You devil of fear, today is the last day that you will tor-
ment me at all. I renounce you and rebuke you, in Jesus'
name.*

I renounce the fear of

- *not being loved*
- *death*
- *pain*
- *the unknown*

- *darkness*
- *the future*
- *nightmares*
- *demons*
- *Satan*
- *losing my foundation*
- *not making it*
- *divorce*
- *lack and*
- *rejection.*

All evil spirits of anger, temper, contention, murder, strife, destruction, vandalism, envy, resentment, bitterness, pride, jealousy and rage, today I renounce you, in the name of Jesus, and I renounce every legal right. Loose me now, in Jesus' name.

Don't stop there. Now pray this:

All spirits of depression, past hurts, stress, anxiety, nervous breakdown, bipolar disorder, schizophrenia, paranoia, profanity, lying, gossip, slander, backbiting, self-pity, murmuring and every devil of resentment, you have to go now, in the name of Jesus. I rebuke you and cut myself away from all legal rights, in Jesus' name. I put on notice all evil spirits of gluttony, addiction, bulimia, anorexia, nicotine, alcohol, marijuana, cocaine, LSD, crack and heroin. Every bondage and addiction of every kind, including to psychotropic drugs, come out of me now. Move out and go to where the Lord sends you, in Jesus' name. I break all these curses to twenty generations, all the way back to Adam and Eve, in Jesus' name.

I am attacking you, devil, and you demons of lust, be bound in the name of Jesus Christ. All spirits of pornography, masturbation, every sex addiction devil, seduction, homosexuality, sexual perversion demons, bestiality, incense, rape trauma devils and molestation, the Lord rebukes you. Come out of me now, in Jesus' name.

Keep going now; the devil and his demons are on the run.

I rebuke and renounce every demon that came in through trauma. Come out of me now, in Jesus' name, never to return. I take authority and dominion over all forms of sickness and infirmity. Isaiah 53 is my weapon: I am healed from all sickness, in Jesus' name. Devil, shrivel up and die, in Jesus' name. Every tumor, infection, cancer, Down's syndrome, stroke [name your sickness and renounce it, and let the devil know he has no legal rights anymore]. *By the blood of Jesus, come out, in the name of Jesus Christ. I command healing and restoration to take place now, from the top of my head to the soles of my feet, and let every void be filled with the Holy Spirit, in Jesus' name.*

I come against every word curse that has been spoken over my life all the way down to my mother's womb. I break all word curses spoken over me and my family by any authority figure who has been placed over my life. Words like "I wish you were never born, I wish you were born a boy, I wish you were born a girl, you're nothing but a failure and a loser, you will be just like your dad or mother." I break these words now, in Jesus' name, and tell you to come out of me now.

Let's come against all ungodly music, ungodly television shows, ungodly movies and ungodly entertainment of any kind (specifically name each TV show, movie, etc.).

Every demon that has gained entrance through my eye gate, ear gate, mouth gate or any other spiritual portal through which I have given access and legal right, knowingly or unknowingly, I rebuke you now, in the name of Jesus.

Let's close every door, in the name of Jesus.

I command every demon that has come out and is coming out now never to return, in the name of Jesus. Listen to me, devil, my body is a temple of God. If you try to defy the Lord's temple, I proclaim God's destruction upon every demon, in the name of Jesus.

Father God, I seal my deliverance in the precious blood of Jesus Christ and ask the Holy Spirit to fill the voids, in every place and area of me, my life and my family, where the demons once had a stronghold in my life. I cover myself in the blood of Jesus Christ, from the top of my head to the soles of my feet, and put a hedge of protection around me and my family, in Jesus' mighty name.

I give God the glory, praise and honor, not only for my deliverance but because now I have conquered my deliverance once and for all.

Thank You, Jesus.

JOHN RAMIREZ is an internationally known evangelist, author and highly sought-out speaker who shares the story of how he was trained to be a priest in a satanic cult (Santeria and spiritualism), casting powerful witchcraft spells and controlling entire regions.

For more than eighteen years, Ramirez has been teaching believers around the globe—from cities across the United States and the Virgin Islands to Germany, the United Kingdom and Japan—how to defeat the enemy. He has appeared on broadcasts such as *The 700 Club* and on networks such as TBN, the Word Network and the Church Channel.

His books include *Armed and Dangerous*, *Combat Prayers to Crush the Enemy*, *Conquer Your Deliverance*, *Destroying Fear*, *Exposing the Enemy*, *Out of the Devil's Cauldron* and *Unmasking the Devil*.

In his first book, *Out of the Devil's Cauldron: A Journey from Darkness to Light*, Ramirez tells of his early training to become a warlock, eventually ranking as the third-highest devil worshiper in New York City. In his gritty, transparent style, he walks you through the dark alleys of the Santeria cult while exposing hidden secrets of darkness. He unfolds God's enormous power through his testimony and teaches Christians, as well as those trapped in the occult, how to combat the enemy and be set free.

Ramirez grew up in an impoverished ghetto neighborhood, despising his father for his careless disregard of his family. He learned quickly how to survive the cold, harsh streets of the South Bronx. But in his search for love and validation, he found acceptance in a new "family" of witches and warlocks who groomed him to become a high priest in their occult religion. His plunge into the dark side reached a boiling point on the night he sold his soul to the devil in a diabolical, blood-soaked ritual. With renewed fervor—and with the mark of the beast cut into his right arm—he actively recruited souls into this "unholy kingdom," haunting the bars and clubs of New York City by night to find his next victims.

His life continued down this dark path until God intervened through a miraculous, larger-than-life dream, revealing Himself for who He really is and literally snatching Ramirez back from the grips of hell.

According to Ramirez, people from all ethnic backgrounds dabble in the occult and fall victim to this satanic underworld and never see the way out. He is one in a million who made it out—and who shows others the way.

For more information, please visit www.johnramirez.org and https://www.enlivenmedia.org/spiritual-warfare-special-ops/.

More from John Ramirez

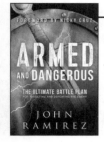

Arm yourself with these biblical weapons and strategies and become dangerous against an enemy that wants to steal, kill, and destroy. Learn to discern and shut down the enemy's tactics, fortify yourself against attacks, take back what was stolen—and more. Here is everything you need to battle the enemy successfully and live the life God designed for you.

Armed and Dangerous

The enemy uses fear as a tactic to torment and attack us—but Jesus came to destroy fear and set captives free. Using real-life examples, John Ramirez, once a satanic high priest, helps you find peace and purpose so you can walk fearlessly into your destiny, dismantling every stronghold, to repel the Enemy's attacks for a life of freedom!

Destroying Fear

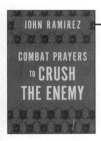

Satan prowls around, ready to pounce on our every weakness—but we are not defenseless. We have weapons of warfare that enable us to be spiritually aggressive and face the devil head on—and defeat him! In this handbook, evangelist John Ramirez arms you with militant prayers and declarations to help destroy the works of the enemy.

Combat Prayers to Crush the Enemy

✅Chosen

Stay up to date on your favorite books and authors with our free e-newsletters. Sign up today at chosenbooks.com.

 facebook.com/chosenbooks

 @Chosen_Books

 @chosen_books